GRIPPED BY

GAMBLING

GRIPPED BY GAMBLING

MARILYN LANCELOT

Gripped by Gambling

Published by Wheatmark®
610 East Delano Street, Suite 104
Tucson, Arizona 85705 U.S.A.
www.wheatmark.com

International Standard Book Number: 978-1-58736-770-0
Library of Congress Control Number: 2006939688

Contents

Contents

Foreword

by Arnie Wexler and Don Hulen

Arnie Wexler was a former executive director of the New Jersey Council on Compulsive Gambling. Arnie and his wife run a consulting firm to help educate the public on the problem of compulsive gambling. Their services include training, consulting, responsible gaming programs, evaluations, testimony, and treatment services. They can be reached at www.aswexler.com.

Arnie's words:

Compulsive gambling is a progressive disease, much like an addiction to alcohol or drugs. In many cases, the gambling addiction is hidden until the gambler becomes unable to function without gambling, and they begin to exclude all other activities from their lives. Inability to stop gambling often results in financial devastation, broken homes, employment problems, criminal acts, and suicide attempts.

The gamblers eventually remove themselves from reality to the point of being totally obsessed with gambling. The gambler will do anything to obtain money with which to stay in "action." Lying becomes a way of life for the gambler and they try to convince others and themselves that their lies are actually truths.

Our society views gambling as "fun and games" and for many

people, that is the case. Gambling is glamorized in the movies, on TV, and in the media. The lottery has become a national event on a daily basis. Sometimes it's the lead story on the nightly news.

Some gamblers may need professional treatment services but unfortunately, there are not many facilities available. In addition, when the gambler "bottoms out," he or she usually has no funds to pay for these services. Most insurance companies do not cover compulsive gambling treatment.

I think this book will help people understand that although compulsive gambling is a devastating addiction, you can recover and live a productive and wonderful life. I know from my own experience that this is possible.

Don Hulen, Director of the Arizona Council on Compulsive Gambling, was kind enough to add the following statements to the foreword. The Arizona Council has trained hundreds of professional counselors to be certified CCGC counselors. The council has intervened with literally thousands of Arizonans who have called their helpline. They designed and provided training programs on compulsive gambling to County and Federal Probation departments, to Arizona Department of Correction officers, to Tribal Gaming employees, and others. Their web address is: www.azccg. org.

Don's words:

Being asked by Marilyn Lancelot to offer a foreword to her book, even though she has asked others to do the same so she might select the one most befitting her story, escalated my ego.

How, I asked myself, shall I write a foreword to this book, which has taken a decade and a half to complete, and without knowing how it begins, what direction it takes, or how it ends?

After some procrastination on my part I elected to write a tiny fraction about the Marilyn I know, and a little of her accomplishments regarding her selfless giving of hope to those lost to compulsive gambling.

I first met Marilyn in January of 1991 when she entered a room where the eight or ten men present immediately turned to look. A woman! She must have come in the wrong entrance, the meeting for women was in the room just next door. She hadn't! She intended on being in that very room and she wasn't about to leave, regardless of negative and sometimes rather unpleasant comments.

I have not been privileged to read her manuscript though I have been informed it concerns her very personal stories and how she has managed to change her life while assisting hundreds if not thousands of other women, in their own journeys toward better lives. The many tragedies she has endured will bring tears to your eyes and her accomplishments and selflessness will win your hearts.

After a year or so she began a Women Only meeting in her Phoenix home. Her demeanor caused many men to cease using profanity at meetings she attended.

In the nineteen-nineties Marilyn facilitated an Internet Web site, www.femalegamblers.org, which before long spread throughout the world.

As the types of gambling began exploding across America, women from the eastern seaboard, across the mountains, the deserts, the swamps, the shores of northern Washington, and all points in between began seeking help for problems associated with gambling.

Marilyn was the cornerstone of recovery for women seeking help for compulsive gambling and her caring set the stage for their recovery here in America and other parts of the world. And Marilyn, may your book be read by all that are meant to read it.

Acknowledgements

I would like to thank the International Service Office of Gamblers Anonymous for giving me permission to reprint parts of the GA Combo Book. I would also like to thank all my friends in the GA program and the counselors who gave me permission to reprint their articles from the *Women Helping Women Newsletter*. Many thanks to Jeff T., Denise D., and Robin R. for loading the Newsletter onto the Internet. A special thanks to the many friends who have helped me edit the book and encouraged me to continue to write, especially Betty C., Paula B, my daughter Kathy, Isia in Poland, and Donna in New York. I also want to thank my family for continuing to love me while I forced them to listen while I read pages from my book. Thank you to Don H. and Marvin H. for being my friends and for all the times we drove around the state of Arizona opening new meetings. And most of all, I thank my Higher Power and Gamblers Anonymous for allowing me to survive the mess I created and to give me the confidence to write this book. All names have been changed except for my family and friends who gave me permission to use their real names.

Confronted by Reality

Please," I whispered to the officer, "not in front of my grandson." Shaking his head, he leaned toward me with handcuffs dangling from his outstretched arm. Moments earlier he had told me, "I just want you to go downtown with me to answer a few questions." And now he was handcuffing me and mumbling something about police procedure. He pulled the handcuffs back when he noticed five-year-old Tyler standing a few feet away. Tyler clutched a little red truck in one hand and the hem of his mom's skirt in the other. My family stood frozen and stared at the six police cars backing out of the driveway. I felt the officer's hand on my arm as he escorted me to the only remaining car. With each rapid breath, my heart felt like it was going to explode. Ducking into the backseat, I looked up at him and held out my wrists. Click. Click. The cuffs were securely in place and Tyler hadn't seen.

I watched the officer walk across the driveway where my daughters stood, their arms wrapped around each other. Whatever he was saying to them didn't seem to help. Juannie and Kathy just nodded while Tyler looked up at his mom, seeking reassurance. I slipped lower in the backseat and struggled to catch my breath. Hyperventilation! I needed to control it. *Control one small thing in a world that was spinning off its axis.*

Everything was happening so fast. It was far too much to be feeling in the space of a single moment, but that was the kind of moment it was. For years I had danced with the devil, but instead of waking up from a nightmare, I awoke in the middle of it. Peeking out the car window, I watched my family huddled together. I thought of my sons…my third daughter and her children…and Tommie, my boyfriend. When everyone came home that evening, Juannie and Kathy would tell them some version of what had happened. They would probably stare at each other and try to make some sense of it. They couldn't. Looking down at the handcuffs, I wondered if my family would forgive me. Could I ever ask them to? I loved them dearly, but I admitted to myself that I never allowed their birthdays or holidays to interfere with my gambling.

As the officer walked back to the car he shot a worried glance into the backseat. Satisfied that I would be okay, he climbed into the driver's seat and started the engine. He must have sensed my bewilderment for he turned and in a gentle voice he said, "You remind me of my mother. She's about your age."

I whispered, *"I am a mother, and look what I've done!"*

The officer put the car in gear and drove slowly past my family, careful not to raise the dust stirred by the other patrol cars. I lifted my head enough to see my daughters wave and attempt to smile. I couldn't wave, because I didn't want them to see the handcuffs. We pulled out into the street, and I closed my eyes.

We drove along the streets I knew so well. I thought of police cars I had seen in the past, cars with some poor down-and-outer in the backseat, looking ashamed or defiant. I was that down-and-outer now. About ten minutes passed, and I raised my head again and caught sight of the traffic light at Fourth Avenue. Around the next corner was the County Jail. The transport took about fifteen minutes. In that short time I began to file away the questions I would ask myself.

Menacing gray walls, 10-foot-high fences, and barbed wire surrounded the narrow street that led to the alley behind the three-story building. The patrol car eased up to the gates. The officer got out and opened the back door and said, "Step out, please." Swinging around, I placed one foot on the pavement, but the other one didn't follow. The handcuffs prevented me from pushing myself forward, so the officer reached in and pulled me upright. He pressed a red button on the wall, and the iron door slid open.

A large, middle-aged policewoman came out and nodded to the officer. She looked me up and down, moving closer until her breath felt hot on my face. I remember thinking I could tell her what she had eaten for lunch when she yelled, "Put your hands against the wall and spread your legs!" I swallowed a scream! She'd probably given this command a thousand times, but I'll never forget how I felt hearing it for the first time. My stomach tightened and I wanted to vomit. I held my breath as I felt her hands moving over my body. A woman frisking another woman was not what I expected it to be. I expected it to be rough and impersonal. Since she could hardly be accused of "manhandling," she freely slid her hands around and slowly patted me down. She reached for a wall phone and said a few words I couldn't hear. The door to the jail suddenly opened just long enough for us to step inside, then it closed with a thud.

She walked me into a beehive of activity and pointed to a long wooden bench. All around the room, officers scurried back and forth, waving file folders and documents, gulping black coffee, and trying to eavesdrop on one another's conversations. I didn't realize the policewoman had removed my handcuffs until she handed me a pair of paper slippers and said, "Take your shoes off and put these on. Someone will come for you." Then she was gone.

Staring at the big black numbers on the clock, I tried to stop the tears streaming down my face. I thought of my boss at the fertilizer plant and wondered if he had reported me to the police. Would it be in the newspaper? I wished I could fall to the floor where someone would just draw a chalk line around me.

About a half hour later, another officer walked over to where I sat. The name on her badge read Officer M. Grimes. She interrupted my thoughts with, "Follow me." I shuffled down the hall in my paper slippers. After ushering me inside a small cubicle, she closed the door and barked, "Take off your clothes!"

I had never been naked in front of a total stranger. Trembling with fear and embarrassment, I tried to remember the things I'd always told myself…something about being strong.

The guard snapped on a pair of rubber gloves while I fumbled with the buttons on my shirt. She stood in the corner drumming her fingers against her folded arms and waited while I removed my clothes. Then she proceeded with a cavity search, probing my ears, my mouth, working her way down, until at last, she examined every crevice of my body. Until I experienced it, I couldn't have imagined how it would feel to be poked and probed with such arrogant familiarity, as if she were literally daring me to voice an objection. A *woman* had done this! Someone who couldn't help but know and understand the shame and humiliation of such an act.

I didn't notice the shower to my left until Officer Grimes turned the water on. She pointed to the stall and said, "Wash!" There was no escape from the room or the officer's stare, so I stepped into the shower, and the jets of cold water raked across my body. While I hoped to hide my nakedness under a blanket of rich suds, the hard soap wouldn't foam. I rinsed myself and reached for the faucet, but the officer stopped me. "Wash your hair, too!" she barked.

"But my hair is clean," I protested. "And I didn't bring any curlers with me."

"Wash it!"

I washed it.

The water carried my tears down the drain. After I rinsed my hair, I stepped onto the cement floor, and goose bumps popped out all over me. She watched me shiver before she tossed me a stiff gray towel. Behind her stood a 6-foot metal cabinet. She opened one of the doors and pulled out a pair of baggy, gray pants and a wrinkled shirt. A poor fit and uncomfortable without underwear.

Officer Grimes led me to a room with a sign above the door: "Processing." There she turned me over to Sgt. Michael Carlin.

Sgt. Carlin said, "Step over here so I can take your fingerprints." He took one of my fingers and pressed it against the ink pad. "Hold your hand still!"

"*I can't stop shaking,*" I said. He held each finger firmly while he recorded my prints. Fear teamed with hunger left me feeling faint.

He pointed to a picture booth and said, "Now we're going to take your picture." He clicked a new set of numbers onto a board. "Hold this under your chin." I knew how dreadful I looked with my hair wet and snarled, my face swollen, and no makeup. He took one front view and two profiles. I found myself wondering which one would be on the post office wall. Because the camera was in the center of the room, I felt like all eyes were focused on me.

When the officer was satisfied with the photos, he asked me to sign papers to confirm the list of personal belongings that were taken from me. Then he said, "These will be held until your release." *Release!* He actually said the word, dangled it in front of me, and with it came a tiny ray of hope. Maybe they would let me go home when they finished collecting all the information they needed.

I clung to that hope as a female guard slipped the handcuffs back onto my wrists and led me to the elevator. We rode to the third floor and stopped in front of an iron door with a tiny window. While she removed my handcuffs, she said, "Except for meals, you won't be allowed to leave this room for twenty-four hours."

I glanced around the tiny cell and saw a small window beyond reach, a steel toilet, an iron bed covered with a wafer-thin mattress, and an even thinner pillow. The bed, a small steel table, and a metal chair were bolted to the floor. Lifeless gray cinder blocks magnified the cold in the room. I looked for a blanket to wrap around me, because I still shivered from the shower. No blanket and no one to ask.

I pressed myself into the thin mattress and hugged my knees. Someone had finally put a stop to my insanity, and now the lies could end. I tried to piece together where or when my problem actually began, but I couldn't come up with answers, so I lay there and cried until no more tears came.

Staring at the four walls, I began to count the cinder blocks. Counting things and working puzzles had always relaxed me in the past. But you can count the same objects only so many ways. If the number of blocks totaled seven or several sevens, it would be lucky for me. When I gambled, the number seven would be a lucky sign, but today I needed more than luck. I needed a miracle.

Later that afternoon, the guard came again with handcuffs and told me I had to appear in court. We walked outside where he chained me to five other female inmates and led us through the alley toward the courthouse. Jennifer, a young gal walking next to me, began crying and asked, "Where are they taking us?"

Whenever fear overwhelmed me, I used humor as a defense to lessen my pain. I turned to her and said, "They're taking us out back to shoot us!" She stopped crying and managed a tiny smile. I found myself chuckling, but I couldn't show anyone I was enjoying my own sick humor.

The guard stopped in front of the courthouse, and we climbed the steps and entered the huge front doors. I hated those two flights of marble stairs. I looked over at Jennifer and said, "About eight years ago, I climbed those same stairs to await jury selection."

She said, "You're kidding."

"No, I'm not kidding. I sat right over there on that bench and watched a line of prisoners hobbling up those same steps, handcuffed and chained together. I still remember how pathetic they looked." And now at the age of sixty, I struggled up the same stairs, shackled to five other women, and waited on the same benches.

Jennifer moved closer and whispered, "*I'm really scared.*"

I gave her a half-smile, and then the officer ushered us into the judge's chambers. He told us to sit on the benches along one wall of the courtroom and wait for the judge to call our names. When he called my name, I thought I heard him say, "The investigation has shown that you embezzled in excess of three hundred thousand dollars. You will be held in the Yuma County Jail until your court date in May, or until your bond can be posted." I didn't hear him say that bond was set at $50,000. But I did hear the word "embezzled."

A picture from thirty-five years earlier flashed before me, a scene from an accounting class in New Jersey. The instructor began the class by passing a 9-by-12 glossy photo around the room, and while we looked at it, he said, "Don't ever forget this picture! This woman was an accountant, and she embezzled a large amount of money. This is what happens to accountants who embezzle." A woman lay lifeless across a bed in a motel, and in one hand she held a gun. A huge bloody hole covered her chest. The black and white picture conjured a vision of red blood running down the front of the photo. I remember picking the picture up carefully by one corner and dropping it on the desk behind me. I could still see the image.

My thoughts returned to the courtroom as the other women stood up, and the connecting chains pulled me along. Back at my cell door, the officer told me that I would stay there until dinner. I waited.

About a half hour later, the guard opened my door again and told me an attorney, Stan Trenton, was in the visitation area. Stan was a dear friend, someone I had known for ten years. I didn't want him to see my swollen face, but I knew I needed to talk to an attorney. The guard walked me down to the visitors' area. Stan looked at me for a minute and then walked over and gave me a warm hug. Feeling humiliated and worthless, I collapsed in his arms.

He held my hands tightly and said, "Your daughters called me this afternoon and asked if I would come and see you. They told me part of what happened."

"Stan," I choked, "would you be my lawyer when I go to court?"

"Marilyn, my fee is rather high."

"How much?"

"Five thousand dollars."

"I can pay you," I said quickly, although I had no idea where I would find the money. Five thousand dollars didn't sound like much when I thought about the thousands of dollars won and lost.

"OK, I'll be your attorney. But about your bond, I'd advise you to stay in jail until Monday, because the judge will probably lower the amount."

"That won't be a problem," I answered.

Stan repeated his intent to represent me at my trial and suggested I make an appointment to see him the day the judge released me. He gave me another hug, and then the guard escorted me back to my cell.

At dinner that evening, the guards allowed me to join the other inmates in the cell block. I didn't know how I'd be received as I walked into the room. Would they be friendly or critical? I felt as if all twenty women watched as I walked to the first table. I looked down at a young gal who reminded me of one of my daughters and asked, "Can I sit here?"

"Yes, sit down. You're Marilyn, aren't you? I saw you in the courtroom earlier this afternoon."

"Yes."

"Did I hear the judge right? Was your bond set at fifty thousand dollars? Or was that a mistake?"

"No, it wasn't a mistake. My lawyer came to see me and said the same thing."

I heard another gal say, "Wow, she looks like Mrs. Cleaver from *Leave it to Beaver*, but she's a real Ma Barker." I shuddered while everyone laughed.

Several women fired questions, wanting to know something about me. "What did you do with all the money?" "Did you travel?" "Did you buy lots of neat stuff?" No one believed me when I said, "I gambled it all away in the slot machines."

After dinner the guard ordered me back to my cell, and as she did, I caught a glimpse of a little bookcase in the corner. "Could I take a book with me?" I asked.

"Yes, but lights in your cell go out in half an hour."

I grabbed the first book I touched, not really caring what it was about. I just needed something to hold in my hands. I turned the pages without seeing the words, and after twenty minutes I heard the sound of a buzzer, and then the lights went out. A tiny ray of light leaked in from under the door. I found that if I lay on the cement floor and pushed the book into the spot of light, I could read. I lay there until my body began to ache. I crawled back on the cot and wished with all my heart that I could have been in my bed at home.

I had told Stan that being here over the weekend wouldn't be a problem. But this was Friday night, and I wondered if I could handle the isolation for three days. I never anticipated my family's desperate reaction to the news that I would be spending the weekend in jail. I learned later they went home and sat around the kitchen table grieving, not wanting to admit defeat. Each of them came up with a plan to raise money for my bail and wished the others luck as they left the house to visit friends and relatives in search of bail money. To everyone's amazement, my family was able to borrow enough money by nine o'clock that night to pay the bondsman half of his fee. The judge then agreed to sign my release papers. Later that evening my daughters came to pick me up. We hugged, kissed, and cried. My thirteen-year-old granddaughter, Chelsea, sat next to me in the car. I remember sliding in beside her and cradling her in my arms. I buried my face in her sweet-smelling hair. While I held her, I experienced a comfort I hadn't felt for the past seven years.

Knowing how dreadful I looked, I wondered what Chelsea was thinking as she looked up at me. "Nana," she said innocently, "your hair looks pretty. I like it straight." I hugged her closer and tried to recall a time when I saw the world as she saw it. My mother would know. One day I would ask her to tell me about my childhood.

No one spoke on the ride home. When the car stopped in front of the house, we all opened the doors at the same time and headed for the kitchen. I slumped in a chair at the table while Kathy fixed me a cup of coffee. For a few minutes we sat quietly, just looking at each other. Then we all started talking at once. Each member of my family voiced his or her own clever idea about what to do. One of my daughters said, "Mom, why don't you just pack up a suitcase and run. You could hide in Mexico."

My son Graham still didn't believe this was happening. "They'll probably drop the charges, and everything will be forgotten," he insisted.

Even Chelsea gave us her idea, saying, "Nana, maybe they'll just ask you for the money back." When she said that, I wondered if she remembered the weekend I took her and one of her twelve-year-old friends to Laughlin.

Tommie and I had planned our regular weekend trip to the casino and asked Chelsea if she would like to go along. We told her she could invite a girlfriend, and she invited Darlene. That night, the two of them ran out of quarters in the arcade and came down to the casino floor for some more money. When I saw them waving from the stairway, I walked over and said, "Here's some more quarters. Now you go back up to the arcade. You're not supposed to be down here."

Chelsea told me later that on their way back upstairs, Darlene had said, "Chelsea, wouldn't it be awful if your grandma lost all her money. And her house...and maybe even went to prison?"

"*I hate you for saying that!*" Chelsea had answered angrily.

When Chelsea shared the story with me, I told her, "Not your Nana. She doesn't lose." But I had lied to my granddaughter.

I looked across the table at my family and felt grateful they still loved me. Sadly, I said, "Whatever happens, I can't run away or break the law any more than I already have...And I don't want to have to look over my shoulder for the rest of my life. The guilt and all the lies I've lived with for seven years have stopped...and maybe I can turn my life around."

We talked for hours. When I went to bed that night, I lay awake for a long time reliving the day. Early that morning, before the nightmare began, I had been standing in my kitchen in my chenille robe, hair in rollers, and kneading dough for homemade bread. While I pushed the dough around on the breadboard, the smell of the warm yeast brought back memories of my mom baking her bread years ago in Maine. I didn't see my mom very often, and I smiled as I moved the dough across the old wooden board. She had given the breadboard to me ten years earlier. I could have visited her once a year if I hadn't spent all my weekends in the casinos.

As I moved the dough across the breadboard, I felt a sense of relief that no one had contacted me from work. Four weeks had passed since John Fletcher fired me on an unrelated issue. And that could mean only one thing—no one had discovered the forged checks I cashed. I began humming "Please Release Me," a song playing on the radio. Maybe my life would be getting back to normal, and I could look for another job and maybe start gambling again and really get serious. But I'd be careful this time.

Our German shepherd, Ace, interrupted my singing with his barking. I dusted the flour from my hands and walked to the window. A white car with "Border Patrol" emblazoned on the doors was parked in the driveway. Living so close to the Mexican border, it was normal to see patrol cars searching for Mexican illegal immigrants. The officer sat in the car watching Ace and waited to see what he'd do. Ace looked like he could tear off a leg before you could turn and run. I decided it would be best to go outside and hold his collar. I tightened the belt to my robe and opened the front door. Intent on helping the officer, I was grateful he wasn't coming for me.

As I got closer to the car, dust in the driveway started flying as six more cars—two from the Border Patrol, two from the Highway Patrol, and two from the Sheriff's Department—skidded to a halt behind the first car. The doors of the patrol cars opened simultaneously, and ten uniformed officers stepped out and surrounded me. I figured they must be here to protect me. If they were coming for me, they only needed one car. Illegals must be hiding in my oleander bushes! I felt so safe with all the police cars surrounding my home. And then a man carrying a paper in his hand walked up to me and said, "Ma'am, I'm Detective Jason."

"What's wrong?" I asked.

"Are you Marilyn Lancelot, ma'am?"

I answered with a nod.

"I have a search warrant to enter your house."

My heart stopped. They *weren't* looking for Mexican illegals. *They knew*!

Nothing prepared me for this. I heard the background music from *Jaws* playing in my head. I should have known it was just a matter of time.

The detective asked if they could come inside. Forcing myself to place one foot in front of the other, I walked back to the kitchen with the officers following me. A couple of officers went around to the back of the house, and three or four stayed in the front by the driveway. The others followed me inside. For seven years I had forged checks at the Metro Fertilizer Company, and during that time, so many nights were filled with terrible dreams of what would happen if I were caught. I pictured myself pushing a grocery cart along Fourth Avenue or sleeping under a tree down by the canal. Just another homeless person. What was I thinking all these years? Now I was unable to believe I was thinking at all!

I thought of my boss and wondered how he could do this to me. Didn't he know I'd pay the money back? I asked the detective if I could make a phone call, and he said yes. I dialed the number at work, and Sandra, John Fletcher's wife, answered, "Good morning, Metro Fertilizer Company."

I choked out the words: "*Sandra, how could you do this? What are you doing to me?*"

With no emotion, Sandra answered, "Marilyn, I'm not supposed to talk to you. You've done a terrible thing." She hung up. I lay the phone back in its cradle.

I wanted to scream, *I only borrowed the money! I needed the money so I could win a jackpot. I would have paid back every penny!* Dazed by Sandra's lack of compassion, I sank back into the kitchen chair.

Kathy told me later that while the police were in my home, she ran next door to her younger sister, Juannie, to tell her what happened. Beating on the door, she screamed, "*Open the door, Juannie!*"

"What's wrong?" Juannie asked.

"You've got to come over to Ma's. She needs us there."

"What's wrong?"

Kathy closed her eyes and said, "She's been arrested."

"For what?"

"Just come over," Kathy pleaded.

Kathy told me that Juannie looked out the window and saw police cars everywhere and shouted, "Oh, my God!" She rushed into the bedroom and grabbed Tyler, ran over to my house, and found me hunched over the kitchen table with policemen all around.

"What's going on?" Juannie cried. "What's going on?"

"*I've been arrested,*" I whispered as I pulled the cord of my robe tighter.

"For what?"

"*Embezzling,*" I mumbled.

"My God," she said. "I can't believe it. Not you, Mom. For what?"

I couldn't answer. I shrugged my shoulders and shook my head.

Juannie brushed her tears away as she watched the officers empty my lingerie from the bureau drawers, check the clothes in the closets, and look under the bed. My bedroom looked like a war zone. Every few minutes they called me in to ask where they could find something. Detective Jason asked if there were any guns in the house, and I answered, "No." An hour later my mouth dropped open when I walked into my bedroom and saw fourteen rifles lying on the floor. I was shocked. I never associated "guns" with "hunting rifles." My dad used rifles to shoot deer to feed our family. Guns were to kill people.

Juannie did what she could to comfort me. "Oh, my God! Arrested? I love you, Mom, with all my heart. I'll do whatever I can to help you out of this mess." Wrapping her arms around me she whispered, "All the times you picked me up, brushed me off, and said, '*It's OK, honey.*' Mom, I want to pick you up, brush you off, and say, '*It's OK, Mom.*'" But there was nothing she could do.

I stared at the graying lump of dough on the kitchen table. At 7:15 that sunny December morning, Chelsea had danced into the kitchen. Just another day. She was beautiful and sensitive, the qualities a grandmother hopes for in a granddaughter. Damian, Bev's firstborn, followed her down the stairs. Being a year older, he didn't dance into the room. They sat down to breakfast, picked on each other a little, and then carried their books out the front door for a routine day at school. As they walked toward the driveway, I remembered telling Chelsea, "You can have a warm slice of homemade bread when you come home from school this afternoon." It was a promise I made many times and often broke because of the trips to the casinos.

A couple of days later, Chelsea told me what had happened at school the morning of my arrest. Nine o'clock that morning, she got an upset stomach and went to see the nurse. The school called my house and asked someone to pick her up. The detective said I couldn't leave the house, and Kathy volunteered to drive my car to the school. As she walked Chelsea to the car, she bent down and whispered, "The police are at Nana's house. She's in trouble."

On the way home, Kathy turned down a dirt road and parked the car. She opened the trunk and said to Chelsea, "We've got to take all the papers out of the trunk." They began flinging papers, folders, books, and empty boxes.

Chelsea said, "Nana in trouble? And the police at our house? I know my Nana never did anything to get in trouble."

She told me later how she felt when she and Kathy pulled up to the house and saw the driveway full of police cars. Her green eyes widened as she watched the policemen searching my bedroom. Papers from my desk covered my bed. My granddaughter walked over to me where I sat at the kitchen table twisting Kleenex in my hands.

She looked at me and then looked at the bread dough on the table. If she felt sick at school, what she felt now was probably overwhelming. Everyone in the kitchen seemed to be moving in slow motion.

Chelsea wrapped her little arms around me and gave me a big hug. I whispered in her ear, "*At last, it's over.*" I'm sure she didn't understand. When we finished hugging, Chelsea picked up the bowl of bread dough and, without saying a word, covered it with a towel and carried it to the refrigerator. She told me later, "I wondered if you'd ever bake bread again."

After the police finished their search, the detective told me to take the rollers out of my hair and get dressed. He said they'd have to take me downtown to answer some questions. Chelsea watched as they led me to one of the police cars. Later she told me, "I couldn't believe you were going to jail! You've always been here to take care of me and Damian." Just three weeks earlier, I had taken her to Laughlin for her twelfth birthday. I thought my grandkids enjoyed the weekends at the casino, but I learned later that they got into a bit of mischief. Chelsea called various rooms and took orders for room service, while Damian ran around pulling fire alarm levers. And I was busy gambling.

Perhaps one day I could make it up to them, but tonight I needed some rest. I didn't know whether my body or my mind was more tired. I couldn't sleep, and when I looked at the clock, it was 4:30 in the morning. I finally fell asleep and woke a couple of hours later hoping it was all a dream, but the clothes still lay in piles around the room. What should I do first? Then I remembered an insurance policy I could cash in and use the money for the rest of my bond. I dressed quickly, drank a cup of coffee, and drove downtown to my insurance agent. Ashamed to tell the truth, I simply told him I needed the money for an emergency. I picked up a check that afternoon to pay the balance of the bail. I was allowed to stay home until my trial, which was set for May. That afternoon the newspaper carried a small article about my arrest, and some of my friends called me. Barbara, one of best friends, asked, "What happened? The paper must have made a typo about the amount of money involved."

"No, Barbara, it wasn't a mistake." No one—family or friends—knew about my gambling problem or that I embezzled money to support my habit.

The visits with my lawyer became more frequent. When I sat down in his office the first day after my release, he pulled out a manila folder and I saw the word "Embezzlement" across the top.

"What an ugly word," I said.

"Yes, it is."

"What's going to happen to me?"

"Marilyn, you stole a lot of money! You could get probation, or you could be sentenced from two to twenty-four years in the Arizona Women's Prison. It depends on the case we build in your defense. First you'll have to tell me your story. Don't leave anything out. And *don't* lie to me."

Taking a long deep breath, I said, "Well, I guess it started about seven or eight years ago…when I went to Reno for a bowling tournament. I gambled up there and hit a couple small jackpots…I won about four hundred dollars. I thought it was fun and easy, and I didn't know anything about gambling. No one in my family gambled. I remember going to a couple of horse races and bingo, but I didn't like them. I never heard of anyone getting in trouble from gambling. After I got home from the tournament, all I thought about were slot machines. I talked Tommie into driving to Laughlin a couple of times a month. And then…I guess I got hooked."

"What do you mean hooked?"

"Well, I couldn't stop driving to the casinos in Laughlin every weekend. I tried to stop…I really did. I guess I got addicted to gambling like I did to alcohol."

"You're an alcoholic?"

"Yes, but I haven't drank alcohol in more than twenty years. I didn't know I could get caught up in another addiction. In the hundreds of meetings I attended in AA there was never any mention of substituting one addiction for another."

"And then what happened?"

"I didn't think gambling could be a problem. I even took my family with me, because I wanted them to have fun, too. At least I thought I was having fun. We got free meals and rooms and everyone called us by our first names." I lowered my voice and said, "*I guess it wasn't free after all.*"

"No, Marilyn, it wasn't free."

"I was OK for the first couple of years, and then I started losing…a lot. I thought it was just a little bad luck. I'd use my credit cards to get more money. I thought that maybe I wasn't doing something right, so I'd read the directions on the machines again. I even bought books on gambling. I felt like I was going crazy. When I came home each Sunday night, I tried to figure out how I could make the payments on the credit cards."

"And is that when you started writing checks at the fertilizer company?"

"Yes. Each time I wrote out a check and signed my boss's name, I said to myself, 'This will be the last time.' But it wasn't. I even wrote myself little notes with a big 'no' on them and pasted them around my desk, but that didn't help either. I kept thinking I'd win a jackpot and pay the company back, but I kept getting in deeper and writing more checks. Everyone around me was winning, and I thought my turn would come. The more I lost, the more I'd spend to try to win it all back. It was really scary some weekends. I would come back to the office early Monday morning, so no one else would open the mail. I couldn't afford to miss a day."

"How long have you been gambling?"

"I didn't even start to gamble until I was in my early fifties. I worked for the fertilizer company for three years before I started going to the casinos. That's when I started forging the checks, and I knew that as soon as I made the big hit, I'd return the money and I'd be forgiven.

"And then on the twelfth of November, John called me into

his office and said, 'Close the door.' He glared at me and added, 'I found out that you charged a drill at the hardware store and signed my name on the slip. I want you to take your things and leave the office immediately.'

"I didn't know what to say, so I turned and walked out of his office. At that time John didn't know I had taken any money. I'd been honest all my life and never stolen anything. And now look what I've done."

"How come they didn't catch you before this?"

"I don't know. Auditors came in once a month to check the books, but I kept hiding the missing monies in different accounts. One week I'd deduct the checks from the inventory, and the following month I'd add it to the repair bills. An auditing firm came down from Phoenix once a year to do a three-day audit. It was complicated to try and keep everything straight in my head...and to keep it hidden.

"At home I hid everything, too. I became a real secret agent and rented a post office box so no one would see my bank statements or credit card bills. Tommie asked me why I rented a PO box, and I told him I was concerned that Damian or Chelsea would pick up the mail, and they might drop something important.

"I remember telling Tommie that we should buy a radar detector and a CB radio, because if we got caught speeding, we'd be late for the casinos. We couldn't afford a speeding ticket, because that would be less money for gambling. I won't be needing the PO box, the radar detector, or the CB radio any longer...There'll be lots of changes. Every time we walked out the doors of the casino, I said, 'I'm *never* coming back.'"

Stan said quietly, "That's quite a story. I've always wondered why you never let anyone get close to you."

"I know...my life was a big ugly secret. You know, Stan, it's weird. Gambling wasn't like anything else I'd ever done. When I drank, I'd stop when I passed out, even if there was alcohol left. When I overate, I'd stop when I couldn't eat anymore, even if there was more food. But not with gambling. When I gambled, I could go without food, drink, or sleep and still keep gambling. I never quit 'til the money was gone. I've always been a responsible person, and it really bothered me to be cramming handfuls of money into those machines."

"Reviewing the charges against you, I see they've listed them as count 1, a class 2 felony, count 2, a class 5 felony, and for count 71, a class 3 felony. That's seventy-one felonies. We need to gather any and all information on gambling problems for the judge to review. I don't remember a case like this coming before the Yuma courts. And I strongly suggest you call and find out where there's a twelve-step program for compulsive gamblers."

Stan was right. If AA worked for my drinking problem, a program for compulsive gamblers would work too. But I wasn't convinced I was a compulsive gambler. Maybe I just didn't know the right way to gamble. He was also right about no one in Yuma having been arrested for a crime to support a gambling habit. I had never read anything about compulsive gambling, but I would have time to read a lot before the trial date.

Stan called me to his office the following week and said, "I strongly suggest you turn your property over to your victim."

"What? Why?"

"Marilyn, if you go to prison, who'll take care of your property? Do you think your family could take care of it? And if you turn it over, it'll make your case stronger because you'll be showing an effort to make restitution to your victim."

After listening to his reasoning, I agreed, and Stan contacted the attorney for Metro Fertilizer Company. An appraiser came to look at my property, and it was appraised at three hundred thousand dollars with mortgages against it for one hundred fifty-thousand dollars. That would return approximately half the money I had embezzled.

Tommie, my boyfriend, lived with me on the first floor of our two-story, Mexican-style home. We had lived together for more than nine years. My daughter Beverly and her two children, Damian and Chelsea, lived in the upstairs apartment. The house had six bedrooms, three baths, a swimming pool, a citrus grove, and about an acre and a half of land. A couple of mobile homes occupied part of the property, and we rented those. Most affected by the move would be my grandchildren.

That afternoon, Tommie and I looked out across the yard. I said to him, "I wonder how moving will work out for Damian and Chelsea."

"Yeah," Tommie said, "they've lived with you most of their lives, haven't they?"

"Ever since their mom started using drugs…"

"I guess when someone drinks and drugs…they forget all about their family."

"I love those two little kids," I added.

Earlier that year Tommie and I had started building a three-bedroom ranch home on our property for Bev and her two kids. Sixteen months before my arrest, my mom sent my sister and brother and myself each ten thousand dollars as an early inheritance. My conscience wouldn't let me use my mother's money for gambling, so I invested it in building the new house. But that would end now.

Moving would be the first of many changes in my life. One afternoon while I sat in Stan's office, he showed me a copy of a report from the courts that read: "It is this officer's opinion that although the defendant has made the initial attempt to make restitution to the victims in this case, the defendant will not be able to make total restitution, given the extremely large amount of restitution, the defendant's current age, and the fact that she will, in all probability, have difficulty resuming her chosen career in light of the current offense. The defendant embezzled a very large amount of money, claiming that 97 percent of which went to a gambling casino in Laughlin, Nevada. The defendant freely admits to this officer that she attended Alcoholics Anonymous since 1965 in order to help herself deal with her alcohol problem. It is this officer's opinion that the defendant was either unwilling or unable to come to grips with her gambling problem; however, this does not make her any less guilty of the offense that she has committed…."

At the bottom of the page, I read: "It is respectfully recommended to the Honorable Court that the defendant, Marilyn Lancelot, be sentenced to the minimum sentence of 5.25 years on count 1, the minimum sentence of one year on count 2, and the minimum sentence of 3.75 years on count 71 of the indictment, all to be served concurrently with credit for one day previously served...."

Stan told me my victim had accepted the offer of my property, and they gave me four weeks to vacate my home.

"We have to pack and move everything in four weeks," I told my daughters, "and Christmas is less than two weeks away."

"Mom, *how can we do that*?" Juannie and Kathy asked together.

"I don't know, but I know I need my family now more than I ever have."

My family assured me they'd do anything I wanted them to do.

"When I called the Gamblers Anonymous office in Phoenix this morning, the man answering the phone told me the closest meetings were in Tucson, San Diego, and Phoenix. So we'll be moving to Phoenix. Tommie and I'll drive up there and look for a house to rent."

"When will you do that?"

"We'll have to go next week, but we'd better start packing right away. So every time you go to the store, bring back as many boxes as you can find."

Kathy asked, "Do you think we should have a yard sale?"

"*We* can do that, Mom," Juannie added.

"Great! I'll start packing, and I'll pile boxes in the corner of the living room." Looking at the corner of the room where we always placed our Christmas tree, I added, "This isn't what I'd planned, but we don't have a choice."

"I wish they'd given us more time," Kathy said.

"We've got four weeks," I said. And so we packed boxes, tossed junk, and piled stuff up for a yard sale. And somewhere in the middle of the mess, we celebrated Christmas without a Christmas tree.

Before I crawled into bed each night, I knelt by my bed and asked God to spare my mother the knowledge of my crime. Our mother stayed single for almost twenty years, until Cindy, Michael, and I were grown and on our own. She married Ferd Swenson, a perfect gentleman and a sweetheart of a fellow. Ferd was twenty years her senior and gave her the first home she ever owned. They lived together for more than twenty years before he died at the age of one hundred. Our dad and stepmother both died two years earlier.

Only two short weeks before my arrest, my sister and I had flown to northern Maine, where we signed papers admitting our mother to the Veterans' Hospital . She lived alone and had fallen in her living room. She was in a lot of pain when we got to her house. My brother drove up from Connecticut and carried her to the car, so we could take her to the hospital. She lay on the examining table in the emergency room arguing with everyone that she wasn't going to spend the night in that place. "Everyone that goes to the hospital dies!" she screamed.

My sister and I tried to convince her to stay. "Mom, Shirley and I have to go back to Yuma," I said. "You'll be all alone in your house."

"That's okay. I've lived alone for a long time."

"But you're not strong enough now."

"I can take care of myself!"

Shirley added, "Mom, the doctor knows what's best for you, and Marilyn's right. You can't be alone like this…you can't even walk."

The nurse interrupted the argument. "Mrs. Swenson," she said, "if you can sit up on that table—all by yourself—we'll sign the discharge papers." It saddened me to watch my mom struggle to complete such a simple task, but she couldn't even raise her head. She finally gave up. I wanted to help her, but I knew it would be better for her to stay in the hospital. So Shirley and I signed the necessary papers at the Veterans' Hospital, kissed her goodbye, and flew back to Yuma.

One week after my arrest, I received a phone call from the doctor in Maine. My mother died after spending three short weeks at the hospital.

2

Unwelcome Changes

When I called information for the number of the closest Gamblers Anonymous meeting, a man answered, "Gambling Hotline. Can I help you?"

"Yes," I said timidly, "I live in Yuma, and I need to go to a Gamblers Anonymous meeting."

I was disappointed to hear, "There are no meetings in Yuma. The closest GA meetings are in Phoenix. They're also held in Tucson and San Diego."

"But Phoenix is 185 miles one way," I said. "That's awfully far to drive to a meeting."

"How far did you drive to gamble?" came the curt response. "Did you gamble in Las Vegas?"

"Oh no! I gambled in Laughlin."

"And how far was that?"

"About 250 miles one way." I understood his point, but I only drove that far because I *had* to gamble! I *needed* to gamble to win money to pay back my employer…to pay up my credit cards! It didn't matter how far I drove to a casino because I *needed* to gamble!

"Maybe you're just not ready to stop," the voice on the phone suggested.

That did it! Slamming down the phone, I decided that no stranger was going to tell me what I was ready for. My family and I would be moving to Phoenix!

Fifteen years earlier, we had moved to Arizona from Connecticut after a car accident took the life of my second husband. My family came with me, because they didn't think I should live alone or so far away. A year later, my daughters moved to San Diego for a couple of years, and my sons moved back to the East Coast. Five years later, four of my kids moved back to Yuma. My oldest son, Graham, and my daughters lived in mobile homes on my property. Gerry, my youngest son, lived in New York with his family. I took each of them to Laughlin to introduce them to gambling. I exposed my family to secondhand gambling in the same way some people expose their families to secondhand smoke.

When the Metro Fertilizer Company accepted my property as part of the restitution, I said to my family, "We've got to sort through everything and start packing right away."

Kathy said, "We'll start dragging all the stuff for the yard sale over to Juannie's carport."

"I'll clean out the carport, and we can set up tables for the sale," Juannie said.

Kathy asked, "Mom, what about these old chairs in the laundry room? And do you want to get rid of those warped end tables Tommie was going to fix?"

"That can all go," I said, "and you can toss those seventeen half-filled paint cans and the piles of old magazines. Chuck all the junk."

Damian walked up to me, his arms loaded with bats and balls and a catcher's mitt. Dropping all his gear at my feet, he said with teenage certainty, "Nana, I've gotta take all this stuff. I'm gonna get on a team in my new school."

"Of course you will, Damian," I assured him. "You're gonna be a big leaguer some day. We're all so proud of you."

"I hope I'll be playing baseball when we move. I really like it." Then he added quietly, "I'm gonna miss all my friends...." Ace trotted across the lawn and nuzzled Damian's hand. "*We're gonna take Ace, aren't we?*"

"You know we're going to take Ace. *He's family*! Remember when you and Tommie found him down by the canal? He was just a pup."

"Yeah, I remember," he said with a grin. "He was filthy and skinny, but he ran right up to me. Now he's so big he knocks me over." He gave Ace an extra hug and added, "Have you seen him catch a baseball with his teeth?"

"Yes I have. But don't throw it too hard or he'll hurt himself." I watched Damian bury his face in Ace's thick black fur. "I know moving is going to be a big change," I added, "but we'll come back and visit. I promise." Provided I didn't get sentenced to years in prison.

I thought about the deposition the detective took from me earlier. "She was either unwilling to stop gambling or she was unable...." Maybe if I'd known how, I would have stopped.

Turning away from Damian, I watched Chelsea skip across the yard and hop on her bike. She pedaled down the driveway with her red hair bouncing around her shoulders. "Nana, I'm going over to my friend's house," she shouted. "I'll be back soon."

Chelsea loved her friends and her pets. A couple of gerbils lived in a cage in her bedroom, a ferret explored corners of the living room, goldfish splashed in their tank, a pet chicken came running when she called it, and Ace was partially hers, too.

Every afternoon she came home from school with four or five of her little friends, and they'd hang out in Chelsea's room or in the pool. If I had asked her what she wanted to take to Phoenix, she would have answered, "My friends."

While we all ran around looking for things to pack, sell, or toss, Tyler looked at his mom and asked, "Can we pack my swing set?"

Everyone was quiet. Juannie put her arm around him and said, "No, honey, we'll have to leave the swing set here." Too young to understand, he turned and walked into the backyard and climbed on his swing. My grandkids and their friends used our yard as a playground.

Everyone pitched in and packed, even Graham. He came to me the day he found out about our move and said, "Ma, if I can stop drinking until we move, can I drive one of the trucks to Phoenix?"

"Of course, Graham." His girlfriend Cindy had committed suicide eight months earlier, and he was going through a period of tremendous pain.

"I know I can do it," he quickly added.

"I know it, too." I knew he'd go through days of painful withdrawal. Graham was a handsome young man, thirty-seven years old, six feet tall, and with slim hips that wouldn't hold his carpenter belt up. If his beautiful green eyes didn't win you over, his humor and tactful way with words could soften your argument. When he was seven years old, he threw a ball at a neighbor's house, and she came running out screaming, "Graham, come over right now!"

He walked up to her front door and said, "Good morning, Mrs. Behrens, you look very pretty today." No one could resist his smile, so Mrs. Behrens smiled, too.

He loved to make people laugh, and he'd make up stories with his imaginary servants: Fabasham, the butler, and Purvis, the maid. Whenever something came up missing, he'd tell us a story in a heavy English accent. "I think I saw Fabasham and Purvis running down the street with it," he'd say. And we'd laugh.

His drinking problem spanned several years, and as a recovering alcoholic myself, I knew the decision to stop drinking must be his. All I could do was be there when and if he asked for help.

We lived in Yuma for five or six years when Gerry, my youngest son, moved his family from New York to Arizona to join the rest of the family. During one of Graham's many hospital stays, Gerry and I flew from Yuma to Massachusetts to be with Graham in the hospital. When we walked into his room, we saw tubes hanging from his mouth, nose, arms, and even through the sides of his stomach. Doctors stood whispering outside his room, and one of them walked over to me and said, "We don't have much hope for your son. There's a three in ten chance he'll make it."

We walked to the side of the bed, and I whispered, "Graham, Gerry and I are here with you. Can you hear me? We want you to get better." We didn't think he could hear us, until we saw tears roll from his closed eyes and drop onto the pillow. "*He can hear us, Gerry! He knows we're here!*"

We left the hospital to have some lunch, and when we came back to his room, one of the doctors said, "We don't know what happened…but there's been a remarkable change in his condition. He seems to be doing better!"

Gerry looked at me and we both said at the same time, "*We know what happened! It's a miracle!*" The doctors shook their heads.

Six months later Graham recovered and flew to Arizona and stopped drinking. His health improved dramatically, and he stayed sober for almost a year. When Cindy committed suicide, he started drinking again, and today was the first time he indicated that he might stop.

While my family packed boxes, Tommie and I drove to Phoenix to find a house to rent. When we first moved to Yuma, I met Tommie at the Western Club where he played the guitar and sang country songs. His 6-foot presence and thunderous voice commanded the attention of everyone in the room. He could have doubled for Johnny Cash. We became lovers and lived together off and on for seventeen years.

Tommie helped me raise Chelsea and Damian. He took them on fishing trips and helped them catch their first fish. When we hiked the desert, he taught them to respect the wild animals' habitat. His favorite comment was, "Remember, kids, they're not here bothering us; we're here bothering them." He taught Damian how to handle a gun and took him deer hunting in northern Arizona. And the following day, he'd take Chelsea's little hand and lead her to the new dollhouse he built for her. They loved Tommie as much as I did.

After loading everything into two trucks, I got into my car and took one last look at the home in which we'd lived for the past fourteen years. Our new home in Phoenix had a small, scraggly front yard, and you could reach out and touch the house on either side. We all knew the furniture in the two Bekins trucks wouldn't fit in the house, but neither would nine people, two dogs, and a litter of squealing Pomeranian puppies. Damian came into the kitchen from the backyard and said, "There's no lawn. Where's Ace going to run?"

Graham started smiling and added, "There's only one tree in the front yard, and all the roots are above the ground. Guess we won't be needing a lawnmower here."

"I don't see any flowers or bushes either," Bev added.

We started unloading the furniture and I suggested everyone

pick a room. Juannie said, "Tyler and I can take the puppies in the back bedroom, so they'll be out of everyone's way."

Chelsea came out of the largest bedroom and asked, "Can my mom and I have the big bedroom?" Tommie and I moved into the room next to the kitchen. Kathy, Graham, and Damian collapsed on the living room couches.

That was January 10. The following night a city map lay on the seat next to me as I drove to my first Gamblers Anonymous meeting. The ride took about twenty minutes. With one foot on the brake and the other on the gas pedal, I debated whether to turn into the church yard or drive on by. I quickly turned into the driveway before I could change my mind. My hand shook as I reached for the keys to shut the engine off. Forcing myself to cross the parking lot behind the church, I nervously kicked little stones in front of me. A group of men were standing by a side door behind the church. They didn't look like gamblers, but then I didn't know what gamblers should look like. I wondered if any of them had committed the crimes I had committed. I opened the side door and peeked into the room. Several men sat in folding chairs around the table. I didn't see any women.

A tall man with lots of black hair came over to me, blocking the doorway with his huge frame and said, "Hi, my name is Pete S. Are you looking for Gam Anon?"

"I don't know what that is," I answered.

"It's for women who are married to compulsive gamblers. You'll learn how to live with the gambler and how you can change your life. They meet in the room across the hall. Is your husband a gambler?"

"No, I am."

He looked me up and down and asked, "You are?"

"Yes...the man on the phone said there was a GA meeting here tonight." I carefully stepped around Pete and slid into an empty chair. Maybe this was a "Men Only" meeting. I wondered if they'd let me stay.

The man sitting next to me reached out his hand and said, "Hi, my name is Don W. Would you like a cup of coffee? Are you a compulsive gambler?"

"Yes, I am."

"What kind of gambling?"

"Slot machines."

He chuckled. "How could you get into trouble playing slot machines?"

"I got in a *lot* of trouble. I lost a lot of money...and I've committed a crime." I didn't tell him everything, because I didn't know if they'd let me stay.

Pete chaired the meeting and passed around little yellow booklets with Gamblers Anonymous printed on the cover. Under the name on the booklet, I saw my favorite prayer from AA, the "Serenity Prayer." The booklet had only seventeen pages. I wondered if they had a Big Book like in AA. The men around the table took turns reading from the book. The recovery steps were the same as AA, except that the members that wrote the GA book changed the word alcohol to gambling and omitted the word God from several steps.

Don W. read the definition of gambling: "Gambling, for the compulsive gambler is defined as follows: Any betting or wagering, for self or others, whether for money or not, no matter how slight or insignificant, where the outcome is uncertain or depends upon chance or 'skill' constitutes gambling."

After the men finished reading, Pete asked me the twenty questions from pages fifteen and sixteen. He said, "These questions are 'designed to help new members decide whether they are compulsive gamblers.'"

The questions didn't require much thought. Number 3: "Did gambling affect your reputation?" I answered yes, thinking I'm probably going to prison, I've lost my job, my home, and everything I worked for all my life. Yes, gambling ruined my reputation.

Number 9: "Did you often gamble until your last dollar was gone?" I answered no to that one. I always saved two dollars to tip the valet when we left the casino. I also didn't want Tommie to know I'd lost all my money, so I'd save a couple of twenty dollar bills and wave them in the car on the way home, saying, "I didn't lose all my money. How about you?" So I convinced myself that I always came home with money.

Number 14 was an easy yes. "Did you ever gamble longer than you planned?" So many weekends I planned a leisurely dinner with Tommie and planned to attend the show in the casino. Maybe even go up to the room early and relax. It never happened.

Number 16: "Have you ever committed, or considered committing, an illegal act to finance gambling?" I not only considered it, I committed years of forgery, writing checks on the company's checking account. The only way I escaped the feelings of guilt was to go back to the casino.

And number 20: "Have you ever considered self-destruction or suicide as a result of your gambling?" I thought of the times I had driven home alone from Laughlin, broke and full of remorse. That was a definite yes! I had considered turning my steering wheel, ever so slightly, into the path of a semi barreling toward me. Who would care? Besides, I was dying by inches every day. Why not hasten the process. My insurance would take care of my bills, my kids would have my property, and maybe the company I worked for wouldn't find out about the checks I wrote. Most importantly, I wouldn't have to gamble anymore. Yes, I had considered suicide. I answered seventeen of the twenty questions with a yes. The last line on the page read, "Most compulsive gamblers will answer yes to at least seven of these questions."

During the discussion part of the meeting, it seemed like a few of the men directed their comments at me. "Some people come in here just to stay out of prison," Jerry T. said, as his eyes swept around the table.

Bill G. looked straight at me and added, "Any monkey can pull the handle on a slot machine."

"Slot players aren't real gamblers," Sam S. said, while he rocked back and forth in his chair. "Real gamblers bet on sports, horse races, and cards."

When Pete finished calling on the members to share, he looked at me and said, "You don't want to share, do you Marilyn?"

"Yes, I do." I needed help, and I wouldn't let them chase me away. I'd been a member of AA for many years, and I had never seen a newcomer treated as indifferently as these men were treating me. I thought they might be testing me—to see if I really wanted to stop gambling. I *had* to stay. I had lost everything I worked for, and at sixty years of age, I wasn't about to lose anything else. I still had my life. After I attended meetings for a couple of months, one of the men said to me, "Hey, Marilyn, if they came up with a pill tomorrow that allowed you to gamble normally, would you take it?"

"Heck no! If I can't gamble compulsively, I don't want to gamble at all. That's like telling an alcoholic he can have two beers."

Before I attended my first AA meeting in 1964, I remember going to the library and standing between the tall rows of books where no one would see me. I pulled the AA Big Book down from the shelf and read parts of it. Now I visit bookstores searching for books on gambling. All I find are books written by psychologists or researchers. I couldn't find any books written by female gamblers.

During the five months I waited for my trial, I continued to attend the six different GA meetings in the Phoenix area. At each meeting the men told their war stories and tried to outdo each other. I couldn't identify with their card games, racetracks, and sports betting, but I could identify with the self-hatred, the guilt, the fears, and all the pains. So I stayed and listened.

"I lost five thousand dollars in one game," John J. said.

"That's nothing. I lost ten thousand one night," Ken R. said, as he crossed his arms.

"I started gambling when I was twelve," said the skinny man in the bright red shirt.

A loan shark had knocked all of Ben's teeth out when he wouldn't pay up. He said, "I started gambling in back alleys when I was eight."

The men swore constantly while they shared their stories. They made negative comments about female gamblers. One night I asked the group if they would try to not swear so much. They looked at each other and grinned. When the next man spoke, the cuss words flew out of his mouth, and he looked at me with a smirk, "Oh, Marilyn, I'm so sorry! I used the 'f' word."

I answered politely, "Thank you for your apology."

In a few short weeks, the swearing became less frequent, and I felt more comfortable. These men knew how to stop gambling and

I needed to learn how they did it. I had used gambling to cope with my problems for seven years and now I had to learn new ways to manage my life.

Every couple of weeks a new woman would walk into one the meeting rooms and some would come back for a second meeting, but none became regulars. I heard men say things like, "Come to my place after the meeting and we'll talk."

"Your husband just doesn't understand," said a round-faced, bald man as he snuggled closer to Barbara.

John S. rested his arm on Brenda's shoulder and whispered, "You need someone to listen to you."

"Honey, you need a shoulder to cry on," Carl said, as he walked Jenny out to the parking lot.

"You're never going to make it," Steve said threateningly to the two new women. "You haven't suffered enough. You haven't lost enough money or gambled long enough, and you still have your homes and a job."

Women came to the meetings and sat in the folding chairs, their eyes filled with tears. They listened to the men tell their gambling stories, while pain and confusion spread across their faces. Most of them played the slot machines, but the men talked about card rooms, racetracks, and sports betting. I was still too new in the program to know how to encourage the women to keep coming back. I didn't know if *I* would keep coming back. One night when I watched a new woman leave the meeting, I made a promise to myself that if I could stop gambling, I would start a *women's only* group. It would be a place where women would feel accepted and be able to identify with other women.

A few weeks passed and the Arizona GA groups held a mini-conference in Phoenix and invited groups from California. One of the members suggested I attend the two-day event and I did, hoping that I might find a female gambler among the visitors. When the day's workshops ended, waiters served dinner, and while we ate someone announced that we were to hear from the main speaker. After the speaker finished, a GA member told us that we would now hear from our California visitors. Several men climbed the stairs to the stage to share their stories. The first four speakers were male gamblers, and then I heard someone say, "Come on up here, Lynne."

I watched as a beautiful woman in a soft yellow sweater and brown pants stood up, looked around the room, and slowly walked to the platform. My heart skipped. She moved to the center of the stage, took hold of the microphone with both hands, and said softly, "*Hi, my name is Lynne H., and I'm a compulsive gambler.*"

Tears streamed down my face, and I turned to Don. W. and tugged at his shirt, whispering, "Don, I've got to talk to this lady. Will you introduce me?" I couldn't believe I was listening to a woman with more than twelve years of recovery in GA. God must have heard my prayers!

When Lynne spoke about her gambling and her recovery, she validated all the feelings I experienced. I knew she was someone I could look to for help in my recovery. She finished her talk with the words, "*The best is yet to come.*" Everyone in the room put their hands together and applauded loudly, but no one in the room appreciated her more than I did.

Lynne stepped down from the platform and walked back to her table; Don and I moved next to her. I asked, "Are you really a compulsive gambler?"

She placed her hand on the side of my face and said, "Are you having a gambling problem, my dear?" My throat tightened, and I couldn't talk. I nodded my head, and she knew my answer.

After the conference ended that night, I gave Lynne a ride back to her hotel, and we stopped at Denny's to have coffee. For hours we shared stories of our gambling experiences. She told me how she'd stopped gambling, one day at a time, attended meetings, called other members, and found a sponsor. Lynne played cards in the Gardena, California card rooms and I played the slot machines. Our gambling arenas differed, but our lying, the way we handled our guilt, and the gambling-related pressures and stress were all the same. I explained to her, "I've always been a good mother, housekeeper, and neighbor. I clipped coupons and tried to save money, but when I gambled, I'd cram every dollar I could get my hands on into a slot machine."

"You're not alone, my dear."

Lynne inspired me to continue my journey to recovery. All my life I had felt inferior and always thought I should do better. "You'll gain confidence in yourself," she said, "and as you became stronger, you'll begin a new way of life."

We talked about the difference between abstinence and recovery. After being a member of AA for several years, I knew I needed to be abstinent from gambling until my head cleared, and then I could begin working the program. That meant doing all the things Lynne mentioned: a sponsor, meetings, calling other members, and staying away from gambling establishments and gamblers. Because I had been a member of AA for years, I knew the importance of finding a sponsor. Sponsorship is a relationship between two people in recovery where the sponsor agrees to be a "mentor" and "recovery helper" to the sponsee. A sponsor guides the sponsee through the program and the steps. My sponsor would also know when I was emotionally or mentally off-balance, usually before I did. I knew I should choose a female, but there were no women in the Phoenix GA at that time, so I asked a male member to sponsor me.

Before I chose my sponsor, I listened to the men at the meetings, and I liked the way Bert G. worked his program. He also had twenty-two years in GA and had been a longtime member of AA. So after the Tuesday night meeting, I walked over to him and tapped him on the shoulder. "Bert, do you have a minute?"

"Sure, Marilyn," he said. "What do you need?"

"I'll be going to court in three months, and I want to know if you'll be my sponsor."

I saw a look of uncertainty in his eyes. "Marilyn, I don't know about that. I've never sponsored a female before."

"I know I should have a female sponsor, but there aren't any women in the program."

"Let me think about it. Maybe we should wait and see what happens in court."

"Bert, I can't wait that long. I need a sponsor now. I met your wife at an AA meeting, and she said she'd be my AA sponsor, and if you'd be my GA sponsor, I could visit both of you at the same time." I knew I must talk fast. "I already asked Betty if she'd mind if you sponsored me, and she told me she wouldn't."

So Bert became my GA sponsor. Bert and Betty believed strongly in their twelve-step programs and lived "one day at a time." For the first couple of months, each time I drove to their house, I would be in tears by the time I got there. After many long talks in their kitchen, Betty became my dearest friend. She would sit me down at the table and say, "Go ahead and cry, dear. Let me know when you're ready to talk." And I'd sit there with the box of Kleenex while she did her dishes. And then I would talk and talk. After talking for weeks, I learned that if I did all the talking, the only thing I would ever hear was what I already knew. Betty taught me how to listen.

Bert patiently explained to me that, "Being 'powerless over gambling' doesn't mean we don't have the power to gamble. It means that we don't have the power to stop or to predict the outcome. Gambling controlled *us*. Do you understand?"

"Yes, but…"

Betty watched me closely. When I said the word *but*, she quickly added, "Marilyn, if you go to meetings, come visit us, make telephone calls, and work the steps, you'll put discipline and structure back in your life." I thought to myself, I don't even know the definition of those words anymore.

Bert reached his hand across the table and covered mine. "We'll show you how we learned to *make choices* in our lives," he said. "And they're realistic choices, not dreams."

"I don't ever want to gamble again. It was such a miserable life."

"OK," Betty added, "you just made your first choice. You said you don't ever want to gamble again. You know, Marilyn, nothing or no one can *make* you gamble. Only you can make that decision."

I worked diligently on my program while my two sponsors answered my questions. Bert's answers often quoted portions of the *GA Combo Book*. One afternoon he explained to me, "For seven years, gambling has been your coping skill to solve all your problems. Gambling helped you escape situations you couldn't deal with. But you'll learn new ways to manage your life and how to deal with any trouble that comes along."

Common sense tells gamblers that the odds are against them, but, as an addict, I ignored common sense. I wondered if I really believed that gambling might help a problem or if I was just trying to escape from reality. Each time I couldn't handle an issue in my life, I drove to Laughlin. Like the night Damian came downstairs and woke me and said, "Nana, something smells bad upstairs."

"OK, you can sleep on the couch for a while."

When he came downstairs the second time and said, "Nana, the smoke's choking me." I ran upstairs and found the bedroom filled with smoke. Graham's mattress was on fire. I screamed for Tommie, and he came running up the stairs, two steps at a time. Graham was drunk. He'd passed out with a lit cigarette in his hand and set the bed on fire. So how did I handle that situation? We threw the mattress out on the lawn, cleaned up the mess, and in the morning we headed for the casino.

Another time I heard glass breaking in my living room. I ran outside and found my daughter high on drugs and throwing rocks through the front windows. Beverly had been using drugs for several years, though she sometimes stayed away from them for months at a time. She had earned an RN degree when she was clean from drugs for three years, but when she got high, she became violent and unpredictable. This was one of those days, and I screamed, "Beverly, what the *HELL* are you doing?"

She turned to me, eyes blazing, and said, "You can't kick me out of this house!"

I grabbed her by the arm, and we began a shoving and shouting match. In the scuffle, I broke my little finger, and Juannie came running out of the house screaming, "Stop or I'll shoot!" When we didn't stop, she fired a pistol into the air and, hearing the gunfire, the neighbors called the police.

Once again, to put the unpleasant incident behind me, Tommie and I drove to Laughlin. Sitting in front of a slot machine always made me feel better. I could forget the broken windows, the burned mattress, and my broken finger. When I shared these stories with my sponsors, they explained that I would find alternative ways to deal with unpleasant circumstances. Five months had passed since my last bet, and May 9, the date for my court appearance, was near.

On one of my many visits to Yuma, my attorney repeated to me, "You know that the judge could sentence you from two to twenty-four years."

"Oh, my God!" I said. "I'll be *eighty-four* years old when I'm released!"

He quickly added, "But there's a strong possibility that the judge might grant you probation."

For my day in court, Stan said, "I want you to wear a plain black skirt and white tailored blouse."

"Can I wear high heels?"

"That's OK, as long as they're not too high…don't wear any makeup."

"Stan, if you're trying to make me look like a broken woman, it's not necessary. I am broken."

The day of the trial, several members of my family and three GA members accompanied me on the ride to Yuma. I drove my own car, feeling confident that I would be driving back to Phoenix after the judge's ruling. Stan was waiting on the steps of the court-house when we drove up. He took my arm and guided me into the courtroom. We sat in the middle row of seats. Bev and Juannie sat in the row behind us, but Kathy waited in a chair outside the court-room. She said she couldn't bear to hear the judge's decision.

The windowless room and the low-watt bulbs in the ceiling gave the appearance of a grade B movie. Except for my family and my GA friends, strangers filled the seats in the room. No one sat in the seat at my right side. And then John Fletcher, my former employer, walked in. He looked around for a minute, and when he saw the empty seat next to me, he quickly walked over and sat down. Seeing the panic in my eyes, Stan stood up, took a quick step to my right, pushed me aside, and eased himself into the space between John and me.

The door behind the judge's bench opened, and the bailiff came out and announced, "Please rise. Court is now in session." The judge entered the room and sat down, while the bailiff instructed everyone else to be seated. Judge Brown called John Fletcher to the stand, and after he was sworn in, the questioning began.

"Mr. Fletcher, are you the manager of Metro Fertilizer Company?"

"Yes, Your Honor."

"Who hired Marilyn Lancelot?"

"An accounting firm interviewed her, Your Honor."

The judge repeated, "I asked you, who hired her?"

"The accountant suggested we hire Ms. Lancelot." The louder the judge's insistent questions, the more muffled the responses from John.

Leaning forward on the bench, the judge stared into John's eyes and demanded, "Mr. Fletcher, I'm going to ask you again…who hired Ms. Lancelot?"

"*I did, Your Honor,*" John mumbled.

"You hired a compulsive gambler to take care of your accounting? Isn't that like hiring a fox to watch the hen house?"

"I didn't know she was a compulsive gambler, Your Honor."

Staring down at John, the judge asked, "Didn't you ever have anyone come in and audit the books?"

"Yes, Your Honor. Our accountants from California came down once a month and audited the books."

In a somewhat incredulous tone, he asked, "Once a month for seven years and they never found a problem?"

"No, Your Honor."

"Don't you think your accounting firm should have discovered this problem years ago?"

"Yes, Your Honor."

I thought the judge was tough on John. For ten years he had trusted me to manage the money, and I had betrayed that trust. My excuse for taking the money was to continue gambling so I could pay him back, not to cause him problems.

Then the judge called me to the stand. "Ms. Lancelot, what did you do with the money you embezzled from the Metro Fertilizer Company?"

Feeling incredible guilt, I struggled for an explanation, but when I tried to talk, there was no sound. I looked down at the rows of seats and saw my daughters and my attorney watching me. My throat tightened, and I literally pushed the words out, "I…gambled…it…all away." And then I began to cry.

"What did you do with all the canceled checks you wrote to yourself?"

Mumbling, I replied, "I took them home, locked myself in the bathroom, cut them up with scissors, and flushed them down the toilet.…" I couldn't tell them about the effort I made to ensure I was the one to pick up the bank statement from the mailbox, so I could pull out all the forged checks. I kept a list of the check numbers, so I could reconcile the bank statement; and then I took the checks home where I destroyed them.

Sometimes I'd be in the bathroom for half an hour, cutting the checks into tiny pieces and flushing them, hoping they wouldn't clog the pipe. How would I explain that to anyone? When I finished cutting, I'd get down on the floor to make sure no small piece fell behind the toilet, and all the time my heart pounded. I repeated that painful ritual each month for seven years.

Forty-five minutes after he began his questioning, Judge Brown read from the papers piled on his desk: "It is the judgment of this court that the defendant is guilty of the crime of count 1, fraudulent schemes or artifice, a class 2 felony; count 2, theft, a class 5 felony; and count 71, theft, a class 3 felony. As to the count 2 theft, the court determines that a prison term is called for. Therefore, the defendant is sentenced to a term of imprisonment of two years at the Arizona Department of Corrections. The victim has received Ms. Lancelot's property for a value of $125,000, and for the balance of the restitution, the defendant shall pay to the victim, $178,049.25 in monthly payments of $100 or more per month.…" I later figured it would take me more than 148 years to pay my victim back, and next month would be my sixty-first birthday.

Judge Brown's gavel pounded the desk with such a bang I wasn't sure I heard the sentence correctly. I thought he said "one year" and then, "Court is adjourned." Two officers came toward me and slipped the handcuffs on my wrists, while the judge added, "This should be a piece of cake for you." I couldn't imagine why the judge would say something like that. I couldn't understand how prison could be compared to a piece of cake. I didn't hear my daughters crying, but I saw the pain in their faces as the officers led me from the courtroom. I wasn't allowed to kiss my family goodbye.

Then a horrible thought popped into my head. My mother had died in December when the ground in Maine was frozen. Today was May 9, and the ground would thaw in another few weeks. I'd be in prison when my family attended my mother's burial.

Once again the guard led me back to the county jail. This time it was to await my transport to the Perryville Prison Complex. Perryville was in a remote desert area, approximately 130 miles north of Yuma and 40 miles south of Phoenix. Being sent to that complex meant it would be possible for my family to drive down from Phoenix to visit me. At Perryville I would undergo evaluation to decide whether I would be sent to a maximum-, medium-, or minimum-security facility. I didn't know the difference, but I knew the minimum-security prison was in Phoenix.

While waiting for someone to tell me when I'd be transported to Perryville, I read the books I found in the cell block. The third day in the county jail was Mother's Day, and a cute little gal, Becky, drew me a Mother's Day card. I wasn't allowed to make a phone call, so I didn't talk to my family on Mother's Day.

I learned later that the guards couldn't tell me what day I would be transported because of security reasons. But at 4:30 AM on the fifth day, a guard woke me and said, "Get up, you're being moved. You can't make a phone call, and don't wake anyone in the cell block." She quickly added, "Wipe out the sink and toilet, sweep the floor, and roll up the mattress." She waited until I finished and then took me downstairs where I quickly ate breakfast before Officer David Matthews loaded me into a van with some male inmates.

Eight surly men crammed their huge bodies into two-and-a-half rows of seats in the front of the van. They laughed loudly as they took turns telling jokes. I couldn't hear them from the tiny seat in the back of the van, but I knew from their attitudes that they must have taken this ride before. For me, the ride in the van represented the first time I had moved and didn't need to pack. The green bag tossed on the floor of the van held everything assigned to me.

Staring blankly out the window where the road stretched north to Perryville, I watched the sun come up over the mountains. I saw the familiar desert flowers, the miles of sand, and the harsh-looking mountain ranges. Closing my eyes, I recalled the weekends Tommie and I had climbed these mountains with my grandkids, and I envisioned the jackrabbits springing from their hiding places and lizards scurrying from one creosote bush to another. I thought of the jumping cholla cactus that didn't really jump but burrowed deeper into your hand or foot after it stuck its needles into you. On our many trips in the desert, we watched the wild horses flying across the dunes and the burros moving lazily among patches of edible shrubs. Tommie taught us about survival in the desert and warned Damian and Chelsea about the dangers of rattlesnakes and Gila Monsters. That was before my gambling began.

I opened my eyes and looked down at the handcuffs and re-membered—my green garbage bag and I were on our way to the Arizona Women's Penitentiary.

3

Learning to Cope

Tucked several miles away from highway traffic, sixteen-foot razor-wire fences twisted around a group of two-story gray buildings. The posted signs along the freeway, "DO NOT PICK UP HITCHHIKERS," were the only indications of a prison.

For more than fourteen years, I had driven past the prison, and I remember telling my grandchildren, "This is where they send bad people." They would jump around and giggle when I pressed on the gas pedal and sped away. They never asked what the bad people did—they just trusted me as we flew past the prison. They knew I would never let the bad people get close. It was a little game we played.

Today was different. The unmarked van crept slowly down the dusty road leading to the first set of buildings. With the clear tone of a tour guide, Officer Matthews said, "Those buildings on the left house the male inmates." He turned his head and added, "The big one on the right is for women." Pointing at several buildings set apart from the others, he hesitated before saying, "That group down at the far end is for death row inmates."

I couldn't help but make a visual comparison between the depressing surroundings of the prison and the flashing lights in Laughlin. I vowed never to forget how the hundreds of trips to the casinos led me to this desolate place. For a brief moment, I saw the words from page two in the *GA Combo Book*, "The idea that some-how, some day, we will control our gambling is the great obsession of every compulsive gambler. The persistence of this illusion is astonishing. Many pursue it into the gates of prison, insanity, or death."

The guard turned to us and mumbled, "There are about eight hundred inmates in Perryville. Females make up half the population." I hoped there would be other women my age, and maybe I'd even find someone who gambled compulsively. Having never seen the inside of a prison before, I wondered if it would be like the movie version.

The iron gates opened slowly, and we drove into a smaller enclosed area, which was the admitting section. Two guards slid open the doors of the van. The male inmates climbed out, stretching and twisting their cramped bodies, and stood waiting on the asphalt for an order. As soon as the officers led the men away, the driver walked to the back of the van and lifted the bolt from the rear door. My legs felt numb after balancing myself on a folding seat for four hours. I stepped down carefully and followed the officer toward the building, through several corridors, another strip-search, and more pictures.

After the preliminaries, a huge female guard shuffled toward me, waved her arm, and motioned me into a tiny cubicle. She handed me three orange jumpsuits and ordered, "Put one of these on. You'll wear these for the next three weeks in R&D [Rules & Discipline]." I barely heard what she said, because I couldn't think past her immense size. She crammed a couple hundred pounds into a tight brown uniform that looked ready to burst. I expected her to begin beating the rules into me, but she just folded her fat arms across her bosom and waited.

I leaned against the wall and pulled on the orange suit. While I fumbled with the buttons, another guard shouted into the room, "C'mon, Bertha! Get this woman moving!"

Bertha handed me my wrinkled green plastic bag and said, "Here, hold this open." She shoved a pillow, sheets, a thin gray blanket, a toothbrush, toothpaste, and a little black comb into it. Almost as an afterthought she added, "Oh, here are the two extra jumpsuits." She stomped out the door yelling, "Follow me!"

Trying to keep up with Bertha, I walked across the prison yard dressed in my orange outfit that hung like a blown-over tent. I imagined everyone watching and laughing at the little pumpkin from a Disney film. My shoes flopped up and down, and my hair was so frizzy I looked like I'd just given myself a third permanent that morning. The garbage bag draped over my shoulder completed my mess. The more I hurried to keep up with Bertha, the more despondent I became.

Trudging along behind the guard, I noticed the smaller inmates wore the large jumpsuits, and the heavier ones stuffed themselves into the small sizes. I wondered if this was done intentionally to degrade the inmates. Bertha stopped in front of Building B and pointed to the cement stairway. I could hear her breathing heavily as she struggled up the steps to 23B. Unlocking the door, she tipped her head to the side and said, "Here's your room. Welcome to the Arizona State Prison System." Then she closed and locked the door behind her.

I stood still for a minute and slowly looked around the room. Off to the left was a tiny bathroom with a sink, toilet, and shower, but no door. And no mirror. For that I was grateful. I didn't need to see what I looked like.

In the darkest corner of the cell, a tiny blonde huddled in a chair with her legs tucked under her. I guessed her to be about thirty-five years old. As she watched me, she nervously bit her nails. I offered her my hand and smiled, "Hi, I guess I'm your roommate...I'm Marilyn Lancelot."

"Hi, Marilyn." She untangled her legs and extended her hand. "I'm Stella Benson."

"It's nice to meet you, Stella. How long have you been here?"

Her little finger wiped away her tears, and she answered timidly, "We have to stay here in R&D for two weeks. I've been here one week." She turned away and added, "I was sentenced to twelve years. How about you?"

When I heard her say twelve years, I considered myself fortunate and answered with a sigh, "I got two years."

"There's not much to do in here," she said, and started chewing her nails again. "We take tests during the day and then come back here and read. A trustee from the prison library comes by twice a week with a cart filled with books. Most of them are bodice rippers." She hesitated for a second and then added, "I read the Bible a lot."

"Maybe we can read it together," I suggested.

She gave me an approving smile. "Sure, I'd like that. Oh…and because you're the newest one in the room, you get the top bunk."

I wondered how I could ever manage to climb up the ladder because of arthritis in my shoulders. So I tested my strength and grabbed the rungs of the ladder. "I've always wanted to sleep in a top bunk," I said. After plopping down on the mattress, I caught my breath and wondered how I'd get back down.

"I'll be leaving before you, so when I'm transferred you'll get the bottom bunk." That was a relief!

We talked late into the night. "One night after Ted blackened both my eyes, knocked me to the floor, and kicked me in the stomach, I couldn't take it anymore," Stella told me. "I managed to get up off the floor and ran to the den, grabbed his gun, and pointed it at his grinning face. He stopped laughing when the bullet ripped through his shoulder."

"So that's why you're here?"

"Yeah, the judge sentenced me to twelve years."

Years ago I had watched my dad drink himself into a stupor. One night after he finished his bottle, he ran upstairs and grabbed my mother by the hair, dragged her down the stairs, and threw her on the kitchen stove. I don't remember my mother ever crying when my dad beat her, but I remember that we couldn't tell anyone about the secrets that went on inside our home. Several women in our neighborhood would open their front doors on Sunday morning with two black eyes. Women were told, "You made your bed, now you sleep in it." So families didn't discuss these issues outside of their homes.

My new friend Stella knew everything about the Perryville complex, both good and bad. I stuck close to her when we walked across the yard, which wasn't difficult because R&D inmates always marched side by side. Guards and cameras watched our every move, just like in the casinos. When we walked to the cafeteria, Stella said, "Stay away from the women who walk around shoving everyone. They're usually the ones who are serving long sentences. They don't care about write-ups."

So I stayed away from the prison yard as much as I could, read books in my cell, started a diary, and marked off the days on my homemade calendar. Many nights I lay awake and thought about my family. When most inmates were sleeping, I sat quietly and stared out the window. Sometimes I heard a coyote wailing out in the desert...or Willie Nelson singing a country song on an inmate's radio...and quite often I'd hear a woman scream. I thought about my grandchildren in their new schools, and I wondered if Tommie missed me. I prayed Graham wasn't drinking too much, and I hoped my daughters were okay.

My daughters mailed twenty dollars to my inmate account, and I put together my first "store list" of shampoo, face cream, and bobby pins. After waiting nine days, I curled my hair and felt a little bit like a lady.

The following week, the prison board transferred Stella to another facility. I moved to the bottom bunk, a new cell-mate moved in, and I repeated Stella's warnings to the new gal. The cycle began again.

After I had been at Perryville nearly three weeks, my counselor, Ms. Linda Woodrow, called me to her office. She held up some documents. "I have your transfer papers here," she said. "You'll be moved from this maximum-security facility to Florence, a medium-security facility. The guards will move you early tomorrow morning." My arms dropped at my sides. I knew if the prison board sent me to Florence, I would only see my family once a month instead of every weekend.

Later that night as I stood in line to place a collect call to my family, I heard the gates slide open behind me. The guards drove into the yard hauling a small cart filled with brown duffel bags. Everyone knew that the prison used the duffel bags to transfer inmates. I left my place in line and joined the other inmates standing around the cart. When it came my turn I asked, "Is the name Lancelot on one of the bags?" The guard rolled his eyes. "Yes, Lancelot, your name's on one of the bags."

Swallowing hard, I turned back to the line at the phones, but the line was gone. The hour allowed for phoning had ended, and I couldn't call my family to let them know of my transfer.

An hour later, Officer Michael Trent came to my room and tossed a canvas bag on the floor. He said gruffly, "Lancelot, this one's got your name on it. Pack it up!"

He watched as I packed my meager belongings. Without looking up at him, I asked, "Does my paperwork say where they're sending me?"

Flipping through the papers, he answered, "ACW."

I knew ACW was an abbreviation for Arizona Center for Women, a minimum-security prison. And it was in Phoenix. I asked again, "Are you sure that's where I'm going?"

He looked down at the duffel bag and mumbled, "That's what your paperwork says." I wondered if they had made a mistake. Maybe I'd be transported to Phoenix and then to Florence.

On June 7 at 4:30 in the morning, the guards handcuffed and chained ten female inmates together and loaded us into a white unmarked van. Big Bertha, the guard I tried to avoid, climbed in next to the driver. We settled down in the back of the van, and Bertha shouted over the noise, "We're making a quick stop at the prison infirmary to pick up another inmate. She's being transferred to the State Hospital in Phoenix. Her name's Rosa."

Sergeant Steve Baldwin drove around to the back of the infirmary, and we watched as two male guards came out, half-carrying a 90-pound woman. Rosa shuffled along in her bare feet, her eyes tightly closed and her head bobbing back and forth. Her black hair was uncombed. Someone had put her orange jumpsuit on inside out, and the suit was soiled with urine and human waste. All ten inmates scrambled to the two rear seats, tangling our chains and handcuffs. When the guards tried to lift Rosa into the van, she moaned, threw her head back, and a column of slime slid down the front of her suit and splashed on the steps of the vehicle. When she stopped vomiting, the guards lay the handcuffed woman on the seat in front of us and fastened her seat belt.

Susan sat closest to the front of the van, and she leaned over the seat to check Rosa's breathing. She jumped back and whispered, "She's got bugs all over her head. There's hundreds! She's got lice!"

Rosa lay quiet for the first ten minutes. Then she moaned, "La Lisa…La Lisa…La Lisa." We thought she must be calling her little girl, but she couldn't speak English. She tried sitting up in the seat, and again the slime came from deep inside her, landed on the ceiling, and slid down her hair and face.

When we started screaming, Bertha turned and hollered, "Shut up!" She reached back and slammed the window shut, separating us from the front seat. An hour later we pulled up in front of the State Hospital, and the guards led the barefoot and handcuffed Rosa through the back door of the mental institution. By now I was terrified.

Watching Rosa's unfortunate situation and feeling so helpless, I remembered an incident in Laughlin where I could have helped and didn't. Leaving one of the casino restaurants one night, I saw a man lying face down on the carpet in front of me. Not knowing whether he was drunk or dead, I quickly stepped around him. I didn't know CPR, so I figured there was nothing I could do. More importantly, the change person downstairs was guarding my slot machine, so no one else could play it. I retraced my steps, stuck my head into the restaurant, and whispered to the cashier, "There's a man lying on the floor out there. Maybe someone should go take a look at him." I hurried on down to the main floor, clutching my bucket of silver, the precious coins that would win the jackpot. I knew I couldn't have helped the man in the casino, and I couldn't have helped Rosa.

The minute we stepped inside the ACW office, we learned that Rosa's story had reached the prison before we did. Groups of inmates wearing blue jeans and denim shirts stood in corners of the yard and pointed to us as the guards marched us to the medical office. The duty nurse handed us a bottle of blue shampoo that smelled like used motor oil and disinfectant. I think it was called LiceAway. Nurse Anne gave us strict orders to shampoo our hair immediately after we checked into our rooms.

After we left the medical office, a guard handed each of us a slip of paper with our room number on it and pointed to the south side of the complex. I started walking across the yard and remembered what Stella had told me: "ACW was a Best Western motel several years ago, and when the state bought it, they stripped it of all luxuries."

I said, "Gee, it sounds like it must be pretty nice."

"Yeah, it's better than Perryville. They added iron gates and built an 8-foot wall with rolls of razor wire around the top. They took all the locks off the inmates' doors so they couldn't lock the guards out. And they've got cameras everywhere."

When I walked across the prison yard, I was surprised to see that the sections of the complex were painted in four pastel colors. The two-story buildings curved around neatly mowed lawns, evergreen trees, and shrubs, and cement paths ran through the center. The south side was pink. Except for the barbed wire coiled around the top of the walls, it didn't look like what I imagined a state penitentiary would look like.

I knocked on the door of room 237. I looked down at my duffel bag and thought it was a lot classier than the garbage bag I had carried in Perryville. No one answered my knocking, so I pushed the door open and called out, "Hello." The room was empty. I noticed two sets of bunk beds and a bathroom with a *door* and *a mirror*. Five minutes later three gals came in, looked at me, and said, in unison, "Oh shit!" They turned quickly, walked out, and slammed the door. I couldn't imagine anything more wretched than serving my time with three inmates who hated me. Fifteen minutes later they came back and looked me up and down. I said, "If you think I have lice, I don't."

"How do we know?"

"I sat in the back of the van and didn't go anywhere near Rosa."

"We don't know that."

I lied and said, "We also got a bottle of special shampoo from the nurse, and we've used it already." After I assured them that I didn't have lice, we introduced ourselves.

Thirty-seven year-old Barbara Peters had moved here from Florida two years ago. Her face turned red as she said, "I'm here for my third damn time! My boyfriend framed me into smuggling drugs." She added with a scowl, "He should be here instead of me." I made a mental note not to upset her.

Grace Miller, a young black girl from South Carolina, spoke with a heavy accent as she said, "Hi, I'm Grace. I'm here for five years for writing bad checks. And I'm only nineteen." She paused for a moment. "I've really screwed up...I'll never be able to get a decent job." A pile of library books lay on her bedside table, so I knew I'd get along with her.

Karen White, a tall, thin gal with long red hair and beautiful green eyes, said she could have been a model but screwed up her life with drugs. She smiled and reached out her hand. "Hi! I've been here almost five years. What are you here for?"

"My name is Marilyn, and I'm here because I stole money from my employer and got caught. The judge sentenced me to two years."

Karen's eyes widened, "How much?"

"Three hundred thousand."

Grace sat up in her bunk and laughed. "Three hundred thousand! What in hell did you do with it?"

"I have a gambling problem, and I gambled it away in slot machines."

"No way!" Karen protested. "You probably got it hidden somewhere."

Barbara was quick to agree. "I'm sorry! Nobody could gamble that much money in a slot machine!"

I shrugged, realizing I couldn't believe it either. At three coins a play, I would have to place one hundred thousand bets, not including the jackpots I won and fed back into the greedy machines.

We talked long after Barbara turned out the lights, and I felt comfortable in my new room. I learned later that Karen had a heart problem and always carried a tiny metal box with nitroglycerin pills. She knew everyone in the yard and told me that if anyone bothered me, like cutting in front of me in line, shoving me, or just giving me a hard time, to come to her. She became my protector.

I felt apprehensive with sharing a room with three strangers with very different personalities. I thought it might create a problem but we all respected one another's space. I knew my twelve-step programs and the "Serenity Prayer" would help me through most situations. Being the newest inmate in the room, I would be the one to make the adjustments. My first question for Karen was about the spotlights shining through the windows all night. I asked, "How do you sleep with all that light out there? Last night I thought a UFO landed in the yard."

Karen laughed and said, "We can't cover our heads with blankets, because the guards come by every hour and check us. But you can cover your eyes with your arm and block out most of the light." I tried it and it worked.

On the second day at ACW, the new inmates were called to the cafeteria for an orientation. Counselors outlined the rules and regulations in the prison yard and went into detail on write-ups. A minor write-up would not be serious, but a major write-up would affect the parole board's decision in approving your release. I found out that Ms. Sandra Rawlins would be my counselor, and Mr. Otto Krieger was the yard supervisor.

Mr. Krieger, a forty-five-year-old man, shoved his metal chair across the cement floor and jumped up when Ms. Rawlins introduced him. Stomping to the front of the room in his black boots, he spun around and said, "I'm Mr. Krieger, the yard supervisor. I'll be organizing teams for yard duties." Swinging his huge frame back and forth, he looked straight at me, "You'll be sweeping sidewalks, washing windows, raking leaves, and picking up cigarette butts." The scars that covered one side of Mr. Krieger's face gave him an angry appearance even when he smiled. Karen had warned me the night before, "Be careful when you talk to Mr. K. He's got a nasty temper and loves to give write-ups to new inmates."

Mr. K. paced back and forth in front of us, constantly pulling at his suspenders and adjusting his cap. He stopped pacing and said, "Your work hours are from ten in the morning until three in the afternoon! Monday through Friday! There will be *no* excuses for not reporting for duties! And there'll be *no* standing around talking!" He snapped his suspenders again, twirled the bunch of keys hanging from his belt, and said crisply, "You'll be paid ten cents an hour. The money will be deposited in your inmates' account to be used in the prison store. Any questions?" No one raised their hands. He began pacing again as he added, "Periodically, there'll be positions open for special assignments. Some of these are on the prison grounds." After each sentence he turned and walked to the other side of the room. "Other jobs will be outside the facility. For outside jobs, a prison bus will drive you to the work site and bring you back here at the end of the day. You'll pick up a brown bag from the cafeteria with a sandwich, bag of chips, and a piece of fruit." He paused for a minute and then added sarcastically, "You will be watched at all times. Any questions?" Still no one raised their hands. He turned to walk back to his chair but then stopped again, patting his pocket filled with BIC pens. "The pay for *off-the-grounds* positions will be fifty cents an hour." Suddenly, fifty cents an hour sounded like a lot of money.

When I gambled, I counted money differently. Whenever I bought something, instead of saying it cost two hundred dollars, I'd say, "Well, it's only two racks of silver." If it cost less than a hundred dollars, it was "less than a rack." Now I'd be adding money by ten or fifty cents an hour.

The next morning, the inmates met in front of Mr. Krieger's shed, which was filled with rows and rows of brooms, mops, buckets, and rakes, enough stuff for four hundred women. He handed me a broom, some rags, and a bucket to wash windows. I took the supplies and headed for the north wing. After working for a couple of hours, I felt like I was wasting time washing windows that weren't dirty and sweeping clean sidewalks.

In three hours I finished the area assigned to me. I walked over to Mr. Krieger's office and told him I was done. I thought he might say, "Good job, Lancelot! You can go to your room and read if you want to."

Instead, he said, "Good! Get a bucket of water and some rags and go help the crew on the east side." Then he turned, leaving me standing with my mouth open.

As I walked away, I muttered to myself, *I don't like Mr. K.* I knew the inmates weren't supposed to talk to each other, but while we worked in the yard I learned some nicknames of the other women. That first day I met Blue, Drifter, Hollywood, Country, and Sparkle.

These women came from all walks of life. Their ages ranged from eighteen to seventy-five, and their crimes included kiting checks, molesting their children, and even murder. Sometimes I felt nervous when I started talking to a new gal, because I didn't know what her crime was. I didn't think I was any better than the others, but I felt uncomfortable. To stay out of everyone's way and out of trouble, I decided I'd watch the bulletin board for outside jobs. Karen told me that inmates sometimes pulled the announcements off the board so there wouldn't be competition for the positions, so I checked it twice a day. The next morning on my way to breakfast, I checked the bulletins and saw an announcement for a position in downtown Phoenix. It was in an office across from the State Capitol, and I knew I could qualify for a clerk typist position. I planted myself outside Ms. Rawlins' office and waited for her to come into the yard. I was first in line, and she greeted me with, "Good morning, Lancelot. What are you here for?"

"I'd like to apply for the position down at the Facility Management Office."

She hesitated before responding. "Well, you've only been here a couple of weeks. I doubt very much that you'd be selected."

"I'd like to try." I filled out the necessary paperwork and walked back to my room, saying a little prayer.

Karen told me five inmates applied for the same position. Three days later, Ms. Rawlins called me into her office and said, "Well, Lancelot, you've been selected to work at Facility Management. You start tomorrow. You'll wear your prison blue jeans and denim shirts. You'll wear your badge at all times. Outside workers are allowed to have three sets of clothing sent in by their families, and you can wear those to work." I thanked her and ran back to the room to tell Karen. The following morning I walked to the kitchen where the staff packed lunches for the outside workers. The bag should have held an apple, small bag of chips, and a sandwich. The twelve inmates picked up their lunches, and we walked outside to wait for the prison bus. The bus pulled up to the front gate, and officers stood on each side of the door while we climbed the steps. I sat down next to Barbara as she opened her lunch bag. She said, "I've got two apples and no sandwich!"

Sandra laughed and peeked inside hers. "I've got a sandwich, but there's nothing inside it!" she said.

We all opened our bags. "We'll call it our mystery lunch," Barbara said. I chuckled with the rest of them and welcomed every tiny scrap of humor.

One day as I was leaving my job, I decided I needed a pencil, so I thought I'd smuggle one from my desk. I sharpened the pencil, bent over and pretended to tie my shoe, and cleverly tucked the pencil under my foot. While we stood outside the office waiting for the bus, the pencil kept creeping from under my foot. When the bus rounded the corner of the building, I reached down and gave the pencil one last shove and scrambled up the steps of the bus.

Fifteen minutes later, we stopped at the prison gate and climbed down from the bus. We stood in single file waiting for the guards to decide how to search us that day. I prayed the guard wouldn't search me, because I knew the crummy Dixon #2 pencil wasn't worth getting a write-up. Each night the guards randomly selected the inmates to be searched. I watched as Officer Anderson counted down to every third inmate, and I counted also. I would be number two in the counting unless he changed the order. Fortunately, I wasn't selected that afternoon. I gave a heavy sigh as I hobbled across the yard to my room.

I loved working downtown. As part of my duties, I walked to the State Capitol building daily to deliver mail. I almost felt normal; only my badge separated me from the office regulars. After a couple of weeks at my new job, I was concerned about gaining weight, because I sat at a desk all day. My jeans felt tighter, so I decided to skip the extra slice of bread and the bag of potato chips. Each night after dinner several inmates walked on the track in the yard, and one night I joined them. I counted the number of times I walked the circle by picking up forty-two tiny pebbles before I started walking. I carried them in my pocket and each time I crossed a certain point in the track, I dropped one of the pebbles. When my pocket was empty, I had walked four miles. Then I counted the steps it took to make one trip around the track and multiplied it by forty-two to calculate the number of steps I took each night. Good God! I was becoming compulsive about walking! And my counting addiction came back.

To stop the counting compulsion, I started reading again. I read several books on prisons and learned that the most poorly stocked libraries in the country were in prisons. And yet, inmates read five times as many books as people on the outside. An interesting idea came to me. Why not write to some publishing companies and request donations to our library? So I walked through the aisles of books, pulled down books by six publishers, and wrote down their addresses. Back in my room, I wrote a letter to each company, explaining our situation in ACW and asking them if they would consider donating books. After mailing off the letters, I forgot about it.

Three weeks later, Ms. Amy Pritchett, the librarian, called me into her office and asked, "Just *what* do you think you're doing?" Pointing to five crates on her office floor, she screamed, "Look at that! Do you know I could write you up for that? I could have you thrown in the hole!"

"I'm sorry. I didn't know I did anything wrong."

"Do you know what would happen if all four hundred inmates wrote letters like you did? We'd have tennis shoes, camping gear, exercise equipment, craft items, and everything you could imagine!"

"I'm sorry."

"Well, now that they're here, I guess we'll just keep them." Then she added a bit more calmly, "You can take twelve of the books before we put them on the library shelves."

"But I can't possibly read twelve books in five days. And we can only keep a book for five days."

"Well then, pick out twelve books and leave them in my office. When you finish one, come back here and pick up another one. But don't tell anyone about this. Is that clear?"

"Yes, Ms. Pritchett. And thank you." I left her office with one book, closed the door quietly, and heaved a sigh. I decided I'd better check out prison rules before I embarked on another good deed.

When I came home from work one night, I looked at my calendar and said to Karen, "Tomorrow is June 21, the first day of summer, longest day of the year, and my sixty-first birthday." Laying the calendar down, I added, "It's also the first time I've celebrated a birthday away from my family."

Karen smiled, "We'll all sing 'Happy Birthday' to you when you wake up, okay?"

With a chuckle I answered, "Okay, I can handle that."

The next morning, a chocolate cupcake from Barbara, a small bag of cheese crisps that Grace had bought with her window-washing money, and a tiny metal pill box from Karen lay on the table next to my bed. My three friends must have placed them there after I'd fallen asleep. The box Karen gave me was the one she used for her nitroglycerin tablets. I said, "Karen, you shouldn't give this to me. You need it for your pills."

"The nurse told me I shouldn't keep them in a metal box." She smiled and gave me a hug. "I want you to have it."

"Thank you so much. I'll treasure it. You'll be leaving in two weeks, and what will I do when you're gone?"

With a playful slap she said, "You'll do just fine. You're a survivor." It occurred to me that I couldn't rely on others to take care of me while I served my sentence. I'd have to learn how to take care of myself.

That night I talked to my son, and he wished me a happy birthday. We laughed after I told him, "I'm so brainwashed I run and stand in every line I see. This afternoon, I ended up with a bag of toilet paper, two cans of soda, and sanitary napkins—and I haven't had my period for sixteen years." In a more serious tone, I added, "One of these days I'll be standing in a line that lets me out of here."

"That'll be the longest line of all," he said softly.

A couple of days after my birthday, I lay on my bunk reading the Big Book of Alcoholics Anonymous. I read the story of how Dr. Bob and Bill W. started the AA program and how they determined through trial and error that they couldn't stay sober unless they were helping another sick alcoholic. I decided I needed to find another compulsive gambler to keep me from gambling again. There must be another woman in the yard who gambled compulsively, because there was gambling all over the complex. Most of the inmates attended bingo games held once a week in the cafeteria, and many of them huddled around picnic tables playing cards. When one of the inmates spread a white sheet over a picnic table, it was a signal that a card game was being played. The stakes could be cigarettes, food, or favors. Gambling was rampant! Some of the guards took the inmates' dollars and smuggled lottery tickets back into the facility.

The following morning I visited Ms. Rawlins' office and asked her to check the list of inmates for to see if she could find another gal with a gambling problem. Hopefully, I'd be able to find someone who had committed a crime similar to mine.

Two days later, Ms. Rawlins called me back to her office and said, "I found a gal who is serving time for a crime like yours." Handing me a slip of paper, she added, "Here's her name." I looked at the paper. The name Fran Martin was written on it. "Fran's been sent here from Tucson. She's serving a five- to seven-year sentence for embezzling money from her employer,"

I thanked Ms. Rawlins, and after dinner that night, I checked around the yard to see if anyone knew Fran. I soon found her sitting on a bench talking to a couple of young inmates. I watched them for a minute. One of the gals sat peeling the paint off the picnic table while she listened to Fran. The other gal sat with her chin cupped in her hands and appeared to be listening intently to every word. I walked over and tapped Fran on the shoulder. "Are you Fran Martin?" I asked.

She gave me a warm smile and answered, "Why, yes, I am."

"Could I talk to you for a couple of minutes?"

She nodded, "Of course." She picked up her can of Pepsi and a small red notebook. Flashing the other two inmates a quick smile, she said, "I'll be right back."

We sat down at an empty picnic table, and I took a closer look at Fran. This is no criminal, I thought. She's a fine lady. Her smartly styled thick black hair complemented her pale complexion. Her sad eyes betrayed her wide smile. "I'm sorry I took you away from your friends," I said, somewhat apologetically, "but I need to talk to you."

"Oh, that's okay. Debbie and Janet are both new. Neither one of them can read or write very well. I'm tutoring them every chance we get."

"How wonderful of you." Fran blushed and gave a little shrug.

"Fran, my name is Marilyn. I used to live in Yuma. I heard you're from Tucson."

"Yes, I am."

"I hope you don't mind, but I checked with the counselor for someone who might be in here with a gambling problem."

Like a guilty schoolgirl, she stopped smiling. "Really?" she said.

"Yes. I'm in here for embezzling money to gamble with, and I need to talk to someone who's done the same thing."

Fran glanced down at her folded hands. "It's true," she said. "I took a lot of money from my employer. I gambled it all away...." Squaring her shoulders, she added, "I worked as a secretary for a law firm in Tucson. One day the guilt overwhelmed me, and I went to my boss and confessed everything. He picked up the phone and called the police, and they arrested me."

"I know our gambling got us in a lot of trouble," I said, "but I think we can help each other while we're here. Have you ever been to a GA meeting?"

She swallowed hard. "No, I didn't get a chance to go to a meeting before the judge sent me here."

"Well I attended meetings for five months before my sentencing, and I learned a lot about compulsive gambling." We spent many hours huddled over the picnic tables, sharing stories about life in prison and how Gamblers Anonymous could help us both. And then one afternoon after work, she came to my room. Her beautiful eyes were red and swollen. Grabbing her by the shoulders, I asked, "What's wrong, Fran?"

She put her arms around me, and I felt her tremble. "Oh, Marilyn, I'm so lonely and afraid. I haven't told you because it's too painful to talk about, but my husband died of brain cancer while I've been in here. It's only been three weeks, and I'm going crazy. I can't even talk about it, but I know I need to."

"Oh, Fran, I'm so sorry," I said. "Why don't we go outside where we can be alone?" We walked across the prison complex to a table in the far corner of the yard.

"I couldn't even go to his funeral," she whispered.

"Oh, Fran...."

"There's a prison policy that when a family member's dying, you can either visit them at their bedside…or you're allowed to attend the funeral. I visited my husband in the hospital a week before he died. I have a teenage son and daughter who are alone out there, all because of my gambling. I should *be* with them!"

Fran and I talked for a couple of hours, and our friendship grew stronger from that day on. When we returned to our rooms, I remembered her decision to visit her husband before he died. My son, Graham, had been close to death so many times. I wondered what I would have done if my daughters had called and told me he only had a few days to live. I knew I would have made the same decision Fran had made.

Fran and I both worked outside the prison grounds and met almost every afternoon after work. We played hundreds of games of Scrabble, watched TV, and laughed and cried together. We sat next to each other at twelve-step meetings. The most rewarding times spent in prison were the hours when Fran and I talked about the GA recovery program and how we could change our lives after our release.

We talked about the *GA Combo Book*, and Fran asked more questions than I could answer. One day she read the twenty questions and asked, "How did you answer them when you went to your first meeting?"

"Well, I didn't really understand the questions in the beginning. Even the first question—'Did you ever lose time from work due to gambling?'—I answered no, but when I understood what it meant, I answered yes."

"I don't understand either," she said. "What *does* it mean?"

"In my case, it meant that although I was in the office, my mind was at the casino, so yes, I lost time from work."

"Oh, I see. Did you change your mind on any other questions?"

"Practically all of them, once I understood them. A lot of newcomers say no to 'Have you ever considered self-destruction or suicide as a result of your gambling?' They don't realize they're already self-destructing when they gamble compulsively." Fran was eager to learn the GA program and asked many questions. And, as

Dr. Bob and Bill W. had concluded, I needed to share what I had learned.

One night the two of us were sitting in the yard when I said, "You know, Fran, we're not bad people who stole money to gamble with. We're compulsive gamblers who *had* to steal money to support our gambling addiction."

She gave me her quick grin and said, "You're right! We're not thieves. We're compulsive gamblers. But try and tell that to a judge."

"In GA they talk about crossing the line," I continued. "Well, I never knew *when* I crossed that so-called invisible line."

"I didn't either," Fran admitted.

"It was like driving from Yuma County to Maricopa County. When you cross that line, there's no billboard or flashing lights that tell you, 'Hey, you just crossed the line!'"

"Exactly!"

"The only sign I ever saw in the casino was, 'PLAY RESPONSIBLY'" Shaking my head, I added, "Whatever that means. The instructions on an aspirin bottle has more detail on issues of concern than 'PLAY RESPONSIBLY' does." We both knew we didn't want to go back to gambling when we were released. We had learned our lesson well—and we couldn't imagine repeating the miserable behavior that brought us here.

While I served my sentence, my friends in GA supported me with cards and letters. Some of them accepted my collect calls. But I needed a little extra insurance to aid in my recovery and decided to check with the counselors about starting a GA meeting at ACW. There were AA, NA, and CoDA meetings and a few other twelve-step programs, but no GA. The counselors told me I couldn't chair a meeting, because the prison rules stated that if an inmate led a meeting, it would be considered leading a gang. They wouldn't allow a male GA member to come in and lead the meeting, and there were no female gamblers outside the prison with any length of abstinence. The twelve-step programs allowed in the prison were all led by women from outside. Disappointment with the lack of interest from the prison system made me more determined to come back one day and start a GA group.

After a few months at ACW, my creditors traced me and tried to contact me at the prison. Ms. Rawlins called me into her office. Standing behind her desk with her hands on her hips, she glared at me and said, "You're going to have to do something about the collection agencies calling here, looking for payments."

Puzzled, I asked, "What can I do about it?"

"I don't know," she said, "but we can't have creditors calling the prison to talk to inmates."

I turned and hurried back to my room to figure something out. With no money and earning only fifty cents an hour, my budget didn't allow money for creditors. I looked across the yard and spotted Jessie sitting under a tree, working on her cross-stitch. Everyone in the complex knew fifty-five-year-old Jessie, and Jessie knew everything about all the inmates. She always listened to our tales of woes, so I walked over to her and said, "Jessie, I need some advice."

Laying her needlework down on the grass, she asked, "What's the matter, honey?"

"Well, a couple of my creditors are calling here asking for money. Ms. Rawlins told me I have to do something about it. What can I do?"

She picked up her cross-stitch again and said, "Do you know Sandra?" She didn't wait for an answer. "She does paralegal work for the inmates and knows the legal library inside out. She could help you file for bankruptcy, if necessary."

"Do you think they'd let me do that from here?"

"Check with Sandra. She spends most of her free time in the prison's legal library. The inmates go to her whenever they have legal problems. She's down at the end of the south side in room 223." Thanking her, I jumped up and hurried over to the south side.

Sandra guided me through my bankruptcy filing and charged me ten dollars, almost a week's wages. The court date was set for three weeks from the date they received the paperwork. One week after the court date, I opened a letter which read, "The court has canceled your petition to file for bankruptcy due to your failure to appear in court on the date specified in our letter."

Shocked at this unexpected response, I wrote another letter, pleading with them to reconsider the petition, because I was incarcerated and couldn't appear. Fortunately, they did hear the petition again and approved my plea for bankruptcy. With the bankruptcy, I filed a total of twenty-two thousand dollars in debts, and now I could concentrate on the $175,000 in restitution.

After the bankruptcy filing, the court notified my creditors, and the collection calls to my counselor, Ms. Rawlins, stopped.

4

Childhood, Wally, Tony, and Before Gambling

With the bankruptcy filing behind me and with my new job, I felt some relief from the prison issues, and I remembered the words Juannie had whispered to me in the courtroom. She had laid her hand on mine and said, "You could write a journal while you're serving your sentence. It would be therapeutic." I also remembered that someone in my twelve-step program had said, "We use our addictions to escape realities or painful issues from as far back as our childhood." I didn't remember ever having been beaten or sexually molested as a kid. So why did I gamble? Perhaps writing would lead me to something in my past that drove me to my addictions. And so in the dark room I fumbled for a pad of paper and a pencil and quietly tiptoed into the bathroom. I didn't want to wake the other inmates. As I began writing about my earliest memories, I once again became the child.

I never understood why my mom chose me to take care of my siblings, because my sister was a year younger than me but outweighed me by twenty pounds. I was a shy, sickly, skinny, knock-kneed kid. I remember my sister not only being bigger than me but also a lot more vocal. The louder she screamed, the more I disappeared inside myself. Being the firstborn of three children, my responsibility was to help my mom with Cindy and Michael. I became a little mother at an early age with grown-up chores, but I remained painfully shy outside our home for many years.

We grew up in New Sweden, a potato-farming community on the Canadian border in northern Maine. Our town boasted a population of four hundred and little else. I remember being able to run from one end of town to the other in six minutes. Living so close to Canada, our parents and grandparents instilled prejudice in our minds. We were told we couldn't associate with French kids or Indian kids, but we never knew why.

In the 1930s our town supported three small stores. Each store sold everything from groceries to cattle feed and farming supplies. The candy counters held jawbreakers, licorice, lollipops, bubble gum with cards, and more—all for just a penny. We would stand for hours with our faces pressed against the glass, trying to make a decision on how to spend our five cents.

The town claimed two gas stations, where the farmers sat in rickety chairs in the back room, telling stories and spitting streams of snuff into smelly spittoons. The most exciting place to visit was the railroad station. No one ever got off the train, but the conductor waved to us as the big iron machine rumbled through town. We didn't have a bank, a doctor, or a dentist. We did have a lawyer who was the most important and richest man in town. He lived up over the grocery store. We knew he was rich, because he had white lace curtains in his windows.

Each year in the fall, the potato crop would be ready for harvesting. Everyone in town—even the little tykes—helped fill the barrels with the new potatoes, and the men hauled them to the potato house about thirty miles away. There was no McDonald's, Taco Bell, or Kentucky Fried Chicken, so our mom relied on one of her seventeen ways to prepare potatoes. She baked, fried, boiled, and mashed potatoes, grated them for potato pancakes, and even made potato bread.

We grew up during the time the government handed out rationing stamps for shoes, sugar, gasoline, tires, and butter. My mom knitted our socks and sweaters and sewed all our clothes (some were made from flour bags), and dad worked in his shop, filling the holes in mom's pots and pans with melted metal. Everything was recycled and mended.

As kids, we could grab a saw, a hammer, and a coffee can filled with nails and march into the woods to build a tree fort. None of the neighbors posted "Keep Out" signs.

Jobs were hard to find in our little town, so my dad spent months looking for work in Massachusetts. When he was home, he would hunt and fish to provide meat for the table. I loved my dad, but I didn't miss him when he worked in the city. My dad's voice was like thunder, but he never hit us.

Consequently, my mom raised us and helped us with homework. I don't recall my parents ever attending church, but each Sunday morning, our mom put on our pretty dresses and pinned colored ribbons in our hair and sent us to the little white church in the center of town. Everyone in church joined in the singing, and I wished my mom would have stayed and sang with us. It always seemed like the people who sang in church sounded a lot nicer than when they sang at parties. My favorite song was "The Old Rugged Cross," and when I came home from church, I would sit at the big piano in our living room and try to pick out the tune with one finger.

Our grandparents had come to America from Sweden when they were very young. They met in New Sweden, married, and raised large families. Both of our grandmas had soft, white hair rolled in little buns. When I was a little girl, I thought the tortoise-shell combs kept the hair from falling off their heads. They always wore aprons, were the bosses of the kitchen, and smelled like coffee cakes and sweet rolls.

When we visited the home of my mother's mom, we headed right for the attic stairs, being extra careful not to make any noise, because we were about to enter forbidden territory. We tiptoed up the stairs and opened the door slowly because it always squeaked, but once inside, we could lift the trunk lids and peek at the treasures. We tried on lace dresses and strings of beads and raised pretty parasols over our heads. If we made the slightest sound, Grandma's voice would come rumbling up the stairs, "Are you kids in the attic?" We would open the door ever so slightly and answer, "No, Grammie, we're not in the attic."

Mom told us to stay away from our grandpas, because they were always busy milking cows, feeding horses, or moving big machines. Our grandfathers had big, shiny, black cars with little window shades to keep the sun off the velvet seats and off our grandmas. They drove the cars only on Sundays to visit neighbors or to the doctor's office.

During the winter months, Cindy, Michael, and I sat for hours in front of the frosted windows, tracing the pictures Jack Frost painted on the glass. We imagined we saw images of flowers, trees, roads, and sometimes animals. The air outside was so cold, our mother wrapped 8-foot scarves around our heads to protect us from frostbite. When the temperature fell below zero, she always said, "Never put your tongue on your sled or anything made of metal. It will stick there, and you'll never get it off." We skated for miles on the ice-covered rivers and listened to the ice crack under our skates. With 10-foot snowdrifts all over town, it was easy for us to cut the snow into large blocks and stack them for forts for snowball fights. At Christmastime, our family walked into the woods to search for the perfect tree. Mom popped popcorn, and we took a needle and thread and made pretty popcorn chains for the tree. She painted walnut shells gold and silver, and we hung them on the branches next to the real wax candles. Winters were fun for kids.

In the summer months, we flew down the hills with our clamp-on roller skates. We needed a little metal key to fasten them to the sides of our shoes. Sometimes we would hit a hole in the asphalt and end up with bits of gravel stuck in our arms and legs. Our mom insisted on applying iodine to the scrapes with a chicken feather, repeating each time, "It won't burn if I use a feather." It always burned!

Each holiday brought all the aunts, uncles, and cousins together to have a cookout in a park, or we'd meet in one of our aunt's houses. The kids always stayed outside and chased each other around all day and shared secrets. Sex was our favorite topic, and the extent of our sex education was peeking into the book tucked in the bottom drawer of our mother's bureau. The book was *The Birth of a Baby.*

All the mothers circled the picnic tables like Indians doing a war dance. They kept busy opening bowls of salads, meat dishes, and baskets of breads, and serving tons of pies, cookies, and cakes. The dads sat together in one corner and told jokes and drank. Our dad brought his accordion and played and sang Swedish songs, and everyone joined in. When my dad played "My Darling Clementine," he would look at me, and I'd blush because I thought the song was about me. After dinner, the dads would go off and play a game of softball while the mothers cleaned up the mess.

Memories of my childhood included sweet scents of the wildflowers in the country air, the musky odor from the hayfields, and the smells from Mom's kitchen. Not many foods could top a thick slice of warm bread with clumps of homemade butter melting between our fingers, unless maybe it was two slices—or maybe if we added gobs of jelly made from wild berries.

I remember doing my homework at the kitchen table under the glow of the kerosene lamp. Mom was always nearby to answer questions or help pronounce the *big* words in my Ben and Alice book. I loved to read. I traced every picture in my Grimm's Fairy Tales book with the tip of my finger and treasured each story.

We had no running water in our home, but my dad installed a pump in the kitchen sink, so we never had to walk to the pump house for water. Each Saturday night our mother set the big aluminum tub in the middle of the kitchen floor and filled it with water. The cleanest one climbed in first.

Country schools were unique. Eight grades of students occupied the one-room schoolhouse that everyone attended, and Mrs. Hazel Peterson taught all the classes. She balanced thick glasses on her nose and wore long skirts and was married to the lawyer. Kids usually brought peanut butter sandwiches in metal lunch boxes. Twenty-two tin cups hung on wooden pegs next to the water cooler, and each cup had a name painted on it. We needed lots of water to keep the peanut butter from sticking to the roofs of our mouths.

At the beginning of the school year, each class moved one row further to the back of the room. The first grade always sat in the front row, and the eighth-graders sat in the back row. The eighth-grade boys carved their names on the tops of all the desks and sometimes wrote nasty things. Schools were safe in those days—no drugs or guns in the classrooms, and the worst crime was when the boys stuffed burlap bags down the chimney and filled the schoolroom with smoke. We all giggled and ran outside and stood in the snow.

Our dad was very strict with us kids but he was mean to our pets. One day some men came to visit my dad, and they decided to rub turpentine on our dog's butt. The poor dog ran around in circles, yelping and dragging his bottom on the driveway while the men drank beer and laughed. I ran away crying. My sister reminded me of the times our dad would kill the cats he didn't want by grabbing them by the tail and swinging them around, smashing their heads against the bumper of his truck.

The home we rented in New Sweden had so many rooms that my parents rented a room to an old man. I was five or six years old at the time, and one afternoon he called me and a couple of my friends into his bedroom and told us to get up on the bed with him. He lifted the covers and opened the front of his pajamas. He said the thing that popped out of his pajamas was his little puppy, and if we patted his puppy, it would spit on us. We all laughed and reached over and patted his puppy, and the little puppy spit. I remember thinking it was funny, but I wonder today how many children shared the same experience when they were young.

When I was six or seven years old, three ten-year-old boys tricked me into following them into a barn near our house. They said they had something to show me. In my innocence, I followed them up the ladder to the hayloft where they told me to take my clothes off. Terrified, I began to undress while they stood around me and watched. While I undressed, I could hear my sister outside calling my name. They told me I couldn't answer her or make any noise, or they would kill me. I stood frozen while the three boys stared at my six-year-old naked body. Apparently my undressing was more for their curiosity than for stimulation, because they didn't touch me. They used their hammer to build a little cage in one corner of the hayloft and pushed me inside. When they became bored with their game, they told me to get dressed and follow them down a dirt road to the back of the farm. I was frightened and did as I was told. At the top of a hill, they made me crawl inside an old washing machine, tied the cover shut, and proceeded to roll me down the hill to a pond. Our parents had warned us that there was quicksand in the pond. When they finished rolling me down the hill they let me go and I ran home. I never told my mom until I was seventeen years old. I don't know why I didn't cry. I guess I was numb with fear and filled with shame and guilt. I felt ashamed that I allowed this to happen. I knew I could never tell anyone, and I wanted the memory of that day to go away forever.

Eleven years later I moved to Connecticut, and one weekend I took the bus to visit my mom in Worcester. She wasn't home when I got there, and I let myself into her apartment and waited. Later that night, there was a knock at the door. I didn't open the door, but I heard a man say, "Viola, it's Fred Anderson. Open the door!" I became a little girl again, and the fear I had buried so many years ago resurfaced. Fred was one of the three boys who had taken me into the barn. I lay awake until my mom came home, and when I told her what had happened, she was shocked. That day I understood why young children who have been abused or sexually molested keep the secret hidden for a long time. I was an innocent little girl and had no idea what to do.

Our parents had many parties where everyone got drunk and fought. Cindy and I would get up early the next morning and clean dirty ashtrays piled high with cigarette butts and lug empty beer bottles out to the trash. While we wiped the tables and mopped the beer-stained floor, we both agreed that we would never smoke or drink when we grew up. The smell of the cigarettes in the bottom of the beer glasses made us nauseous.

When I reached the age of eleven, our lives changed. Our parents drank and fought more often. Each time they fought, Cindy, Michael, and I hid in the back of the closet with our fists pressed to our ears, trying to shut out the noise. One night my dad grabbed my mother by her hair and dragged her down the stairs. He shoved her against the stove and wouldn't stop beating her. I grabbed a chair and slammed it on his back. When morning came, everyone pretended nothing had happened the night before. So many secrets for a little girl to remember and try to forget at the same time.

When I couldn't watch the fighting any longer, I begged my mom, "If you don't leave Dad, I'm going to run away from home." She filed for a divorce shortly after, and the courts granted her custody of the three of us. My dad remarried, and we became one big unhappy family. When my mom heard Dad had remarried, she began drinking again, and when Dad took her to court, the judge granted him custody of the three of us.

One Saturday morning our dad gave us ten dollars to take the bus into Worcester to buy three pairs of jeans. The bus drove by White City, a huge amusement park, and I suggested we stop for fifteen minutes and take one ride on the roller coaster. Cindy and Michael both agreed, and we took one ride. Then I said, "Let's spend one whole dollar and ride two more times. It's only ten cents a ride." Again Cindy and Michael agreed. We climbed back on the roller coaster for a couple more rides. "Well, we've spent a whole dollar now," I said. "What do you think about spending each a dollar, which would be two more dollars and six more rides? We'll still have seven dollars for jeans." Again they agreed.

We became so familiar with the steel tracks we didn't even have to hang on going around the sharp turns or down the dips and up the steep climbs. "Why not spend five dollars, and maybe we could go visit Mom in Worcester, and she'd give us the five dollars for jeans." Again they agreed with their older sister. After that money was gone, I said, "Mom would give us the whole ten dollars for jeans if we tell her what we've done." So we stayed on the roller coaster until the ten dollars was gone, got on the bus, and convinced our mother to reimburse us the ten dollars. We bought the jeans and caught another bus home. Dad was so proud of the great job we'd done.

After I finished my junior year in high school, Dad moved us back to Maine. Our hearts were broken, because we wouldn't be able to visit our mother. I remember that day as one of the saddest days in my life. We didn't like our new stepmother. She was skinny and had big boobs and hollered all the time, a regular Cinderella stepmother. She didn't like Michael and sometimes beat him with the broom.

Being painfully shy in school, I never played sports or joined clubs, so that left me with plenty of time to concentrate on classes. I excelled academically and remained at the top of my class, but I never won any popularity contests. I remember during one of my lunch hours, I walked over to where my sister stood with her friends. She laughed at me and said, "Go away! Go find your own friends—these are my friends." I didn't have any friends. I was shy and skinny with a bubble butt and didn't gain any weight until the doctor removed my tonsils at the age of fifteen.

I loved school and always got *A*s but never had enough confidence to raise my hand in front of the class to volunteer an answer to a question. My inferiority complex lasted until I reached my mid-thirties. It was so crippling I couldn't participate in an innocent conversation or walk across a crowded room.

Even with my low self-esteem, I wanted desperately to go to college. I remember one afternoon when my uncle visited us, and I heard a conversation between him and my dad. My uncle said, "If you take your kids out of school to work on the farm, I'll take mine out, too." I told my dad later that I would run away from home if he took me out of school. He allowed me to remain in school.

In my senior year, I sent away for college brochures and studied them in my room. One day I mustered up the courage and said, "Dad, I want to go to college."

He stopped me short with, "Girls don't need college! You get married and raise a family." Then he added, "End of discussion!" One month after graduation, at the age of seventeen, I bought a train ticket and headed for Connecticut. I knew I would never return to New Sweden again. I rented a room at the YWCA and applied for a position at an insurance company. After taking the typing test, the interviewer politely told me, "I'm sorry, but seventeen words per minute doesn't qualify for the job."

I desperately needed work, so I asked, "If you can find anything for me to do, I'll go to night school and increase my typing speed." I took a deep breath and added, "I really have to find a job."

She must have taken pity on me. "Well," she said, "we can put you in a position as a runner. You'd work for the auditors and run back and forth to the file room for documents. We can keep you in that position until you increase your typing skills." It took me two months to move up to the typing pool.

During this time I met Beverly at the YWCA. Beverly was a model from the Midwest, and she became my *first* best friend. She introduced me to some of the great classical artists. We listened to records in our room for hours. Each weekend we rode the bus to Ocean Beach in New London and returned with beautiful tanned bodies. We met all the lifeguards and had wonderful times. One weekend the lifeguards had a contest and voted Beverly as having the prettiest bust on the beach. She told me that they voted me as having the best butt on the beach. I cried for hours, until she convinced me it was a compliment. She introduced me to tampons one weekend, so I could go in swimming. I wasted a half box of those little cardboard tubes before I knew what I was doing or where they were supposed to go.

Each night when I walked home from my typing class, I promised myself I'd never make the same mistakes my parents made. But then one Saturday night at a dance, I met a young man who didn't drink. David was a handsome young Irish fellow who danced his way into my heart. He was a carpenter and a prizefighter, and he worked hard.

In 1951 I converted to Catholicism, and David and I married. Becoming Catholic added a guilt problem to my inferiority complex. Now I had guilt from the religious teachings, feelings of inferiority, and I was a pro at keeping secrets. This was a time when "good girls" never got pregnant before they married, and they *never* asked questions about sex. Whenever I asked my mother a question about sex, the answer was always the same: "Shhh, we don't talk about things like that in the kitchen." Well, it turned out that we didn't talk about things like that in any room of the house. My mother gave me two more pearls of wisdom: "Don't ever cut the tags off mattresses (under penalty of law)," and "Always wear clean underwear in case you get in an accident." David and I had five children within six and a half years, exactly what I had moved from New Sweden to avoid. Unknowingly, I had followed the advice of my dad: "*Get married and raise a family.*" I didn't get pregnant five times in six years to fulfill a purpose; I didn't know how to stop.

After the birth of our second child, we moved into a white Cape Cod between a pink ranch house and a blue split-level. Like all our neighbors, we put two bright aluminum garbage pails at the curb twice a week, planted petunias around our porch, and parked a station wagon in our driveway. Sundays, we piled our families into our station wagons and drove to church. After church we sat at our tables and enjoyed dinner as a family. The Joneses kept up with the Smiths, and we were all carbon copies of each other.

Life was good. Five years later we moved to a five-bedroom home with a swimming pool in an upscale neighborhood. I stayed home and took care of the family and planted flower gardens. Our family had the usual childhood traumas: sudden trips to the emergency room, broken bones, moth in the ear, fishhooks in the eyelid, bumps and bruises, and sunburns. I kept busy driving the kids to baseball and football games. I also became a Scout leader, carpooled with neighbors for school events, and assumed all the parental obligations expected of a mother. Like all the mothers in the neighborhood, I watched the weekly soap operas. I became part of the soap opera families and laughed and cried with the actors. I was a soap opera junkie. David spent most of his time away from home playing golf or softball or working at the car lots we owned.

Because my husband was away most of the time, our marriage became strained, and we both started to drink. David drank after work with his buddies, and I used alcohol to go to sleep when David didn't come home. Some nights he tiptoed into our bedroom with a story that he had been selling cars to the men in the bars. He said, "It's the only time I can talk to some of these customers." He always promised, "This is the last time I'll stay out late." The very next night, I'd fix my hair, put on my makeup, cook a great dinner, and wait for him. Two hours later, I'd wash the makeup off, put the food in the refrigerator, mix a couple of drinks, and go to bed. I soon found myself drinking a couple of beers in the morning to chase away the shakes.

Because I was a closet drinker, I prided myself on never getting drunk in public. When we came home from a party, I'd reach into the back of the kitchen cabinet and retrieve my bottle. I hid it because David started marking the bottle to check how much I drank. When I saw the lines he drew, I said, "If you didn't watch me, I wouldn't drink so much. By spying on me, you force me to hide my bottle." Several times when I noticed the lines he drew, I would add five or six more lines. Bourbon was my drink of choice, but when I ran out, I reached for the vanilla bottle or took a swig of paregoric.

My drinking began shortly after our fifth baby was born, and I drank for seven years. When I got drunk, I became paranoid and would hide by crawling behind the couch or in the back of the closet, or I'd lie down somewhere and cover myself with piles of clothing. Once I took a pillow and blanket and crawled out the window onto the roof to sleep.

One day I looked in the mirror and didn't recognize the stranger with bloated features, tangled hair, and vacant eyes. Still I continued to drink, throw up, hallucinate, and go through withdrawals. I knew nothing about alcoholism. At one period in my alcoholic drinking, I experimented with NyQuil and became hooked on the cough medicine. The cold just never got better. To this day, I can't walk past a NyQuil display in a drugstore without gagging.

I contemplated suicide several times, and one night I slipped into a pretty nightgown and stumbled to the swimming pool to end it all. The next day the newspaper headlines would read, "Woman drowns in backyard pool." The photographer would take a picture of me from under the water, floating in my pink negligee. I didn't really want to die, but I knew I couldn't go on this way much longer.

Later that year I was scheduled to go into the hospital for six days for a varicose vein operation. I was proud of myself for not wanting to drink while I lay in the hospital bed. I didn't realize at the time that I was being fed pain medication. A pill to an alcoholic is like a drink in capsule form. When the hospital released me, they didn't send any pills home with me, and the compulsion for a drink returned. With both legs stiff and wrapped in elastic bandages, I hobbled out to the car to test my legs on the brakes and the gas pedal. I wanted to be sure I could stop the car in case of an emergency. My sister-in-law didn't have a driver's license but rode with me to buy some whiskey. I was so desperate for a drink, I couldn't think sensibly, and the obsession to drink won again.

During the final two years of my drinking, thoughts of suicide kept recurring. Filled with loneliness and terribly confused, I visited our parish priest. In the dark of the confessional booth, I confessed my problem. The priest asked me why I drank so much, and I answered, "I don't know."

He said, "Don't drink so much."

Finding no help from the priest, I made an appointment with my family physician. I lied to my doctor about how much or how often I drank. He asked me, "Why do you drink so much?"

Again I answered, "I don't know." He listened patiently to my story and prescribed Librium. He told me not to drink alcohol while taking the tranquilizers, and I followed his instructions for two months. That was the year Lee Harvey Oswald assassinated President John F. Kennedy, and that afternoon I washed the Librium down with bourbon.

A few weeks later, I sat alone at my kitchen table with an empty bourbon bottle in front of me and realized the alcohol wasn't working. What would I do if I couldn't escape into the bottle. That afternoon in 1964, I reached for the phone book and looked up the number to Alcoholics Anonymous. A sweet voice on the other end of the line said, "Are you having a problem with alcohol?"

Sobbing, I answered, "Yes, I am."

"There's a meeting tomorrow morning in West Hartford." She gave me directions to the meeting, and I remember I lay awake all night. By about 5 AM, I was shaking and gagging, so I took a couple of Librium and a few shots of bourbon. Too sick to drive the next morning, I asked David if he would take me to the meeting.

The meeting was about twelve miles away, and David lectured me all the way. "You don't need to go to meetings...just cut down a little."

"I've got to try the meeting. I'm so sick and scared."

David waited in the car outside the meeting, and when I came out, he asked, "What happened? What did they say to you?"

"I don't know, but I know that whatever it was, it made me feel better...and I know I'm coming back." I knew my husband would never understand my feelings that morning. He fought my attempt to attend meetings, and one night he followed my friends and me on our way home from a meeting and tried to force our car off the road.

Although my husband didn't understand the alcohol addiction, I thought I might be able to explain my drinking problem to my five children. I wanted them to know why I sometimes acted strange. After attending several meetings, I shared some topics with them that I thought they'd understand. I told them that when I got thirsty, I needed to have a cold glass of Coca-Cola in the refrigerator, so I wouldn't think about having a drink of alcohol. We would go to the grocery store and come home with six big bottles of Coke (for Mom), and before I put all the groceries away, five bottles of Coke would disappear. Each kid took one bottle and hid it, so when I needed a Coke, they'd run and get a bottle and say, "Here, Mom, I've got some Coke for you." They helped me stay away from alcohol. I've heard it said so many times, and I've said it myself, "Kids don't understand," but I think they do.

During the last ten years of our marriage, we had many all-night arguments, but no knockdown fights. My husband spent all our money on parties at the local bars. One day we received a letter from the mortgage company, notifying us that they were repossessing our home. David cosigned loans for his barroom buddies and used our home as collateral. The bank refinanced our home and added the outstanding loans, and they allowed us to stay in our house.

Later that year, David was missing for six or seven days, both at the dealership and at home. When the salesmen asked me to come down to run the office, I convinced them to stick to their regular routines and assured them David would be home soon. That weekend while I was working in my kitchen, the door opened and in walked my husband. With wrinkled and soiled clothes and bloodshot eyes, he was a mess as he stumbled across the kitchen. "My God! Where have you been?" I asked.

"I've been in New York buying cars."

"Why didn't you call? We've been worried that something had happened to you."

"You knew I was okay."

I grabbed an airplane ticket sticking out of his jacket pocket and saw it was a round-trip plane ticket to Florida. I knew this was the end. I stopped drinking with the help of my new support group and followed their suggestion to not make any drastic changes for one year. At the end of the year, I hired a lawyer and divorced my husband. David continued to drink, and because of his drinking, we lost the car agency, and he was unable to provide child support or alimony. The mortgage company evicted us from our home. After nineteen years of marriage, I had no home, and I had five children to raise by myself.

We moved into a smaller house, and I applied for welfare assistance. I fed my family with the help of food stamps. Our oldest daughter, Kathy, was fifteen at the time, and the youngest, Gerry, was eight and a half. I went to work for the first time in sixteen years, as a part-time receptionist. Teaching myself bookkeeping, I was fortunate to find a job that paid barely enough to support my family.

I was repeating the cycle my mother had gone through so many years ago. I found an inner strength when I remembered how my mother found the courage to raise three kids by herself. A year after my divorce from David, my friends encouraged me to attend a Parents Without Partners dance. This would be my first dating experience in nineteen years, and I was still angry at men. Squirming in my chair, I thought of dozens of places I'd rather be than dancing with strangers. When the band leader announced, "Ladies' choice for this dance," my eyes sought out the man standing in the dark corner across the room. I decided if I'd ask any man to dance, it would be him. He had broad shoulders, beautiful brown wavy hair, a beard and moustache, and gorgeous brown eyes. He reminded me of a knight in shining armor. I had noticed earlier in the evening that all the ladies asked him to dance, and he said no each time. I asked him to dance, and he said yes! Later he told my friends that I knocked three people down when I dashed madly across the room.

We danced around the floor, and magic filled the air. Wally told me that he had divorced his wife a year ago. I invited him to join my friends and me for breakfast. "Wait a minute," I said. "I don't even know your last name."

"You'll laugh if I tell you."

"No, I won't."

"Yes, you will."

"I promise I won't."

"It's Lancelot."

I started laughing. "See, I told you you'd laugh," he said.

"But Camelot is my very favorite story!"

And then about fourteen months after the divorce, I fell in love again. I was an attractive woman and had a way with words, and between marriages I used my feminine wiles to entice men to fall in love with me. When they did, I became bored and chased them away. Today I look back and wonder if I ever knew what love was.

Wally was thirteen years younger than me. Within two years we married and honeymooned at Myrtle Beach, South Carolina. The first year we were together, we flew to Portugal for a vacation. Wally assumed responsibility for my children, and we bought a beautiful home on the side of a 20-acre hill in Coventry, Connecticut. It was to be our Camelot.

The neighbors lived far apart, and everyone drove trucks and talked about raising animals. The men chewed snuff. We planted a huge vegetable garden, raised pigs, chickens, steer, ducks, and anything we could catch and keep inside a fence. The chickens laid eggs, the pigs dug holes, and the steer tore the fences down.

One afternoon a man knocked on our front door and said, "Mrs. Lancelot, did you know one of your pigs is running up and down the road?"

With a twinkle in my eye, I replied, "Yes, he's a road hog."

Another time a man came to the house and hollered, "Your damn steer is ruining my corn crop!"

I answered, "He can't be! He's inside the electric fence."

"Well, follow me!"

I followed him across the road. There in the middle of the cornfield, hiding between two rows of 6-foot-tall corn, one of our steers

stood staring at me. He looked really guilty, with an ear of corn
hanging from the corner of his mouth. I apologized to our neighbor and led the steer back to our yard. Sometimes it seemed like
our animals became house pets. We had a large chicken that stole
its way into the house several times, preferring to sit on the living
room couch. I would grab the broom and chase the chicken back
outside. More than once, our baby calf could be found standing on
the front steps, looking in the screen door.

Marriage to Wally left me with some of the most memorable
times in my life.

Our Camelot romance didn't last. Wally was an ironworker,
and his job took him to other states. One of his assignments was
in Maine to work on a tunnel. I was lonely when he was away
and always afraid that one day he might not come back. When
he left that Sunday afternoon, he promised me he would never
work out of state again. It had been less than three years since we
had moved into our new home, when on July 6, 1976, my oldest
daughter, Kathy, heard me open the front door and called me into
the kitchen. She choked out the words that shattered my world,
"Mom, Wally's been killed in a car accident in Maine."

I remember screaming and beating her on the head saying,
"Don't say he's dead! Say he's hurt…or something, but don't say he's dead!"
I don't remember grabbing her, but she said I threw her across the
room. She jumped up and put her arms around me and I collapsed.
Around a blind corner on a back road, a tire had blown out, and
two trucks had crashed head-on killing three people. Wally, at the
age of thirty-two, died instantly, and I was alone again.

Everyone loved Wally. Hundreds of friends and family crowded the funeral home. The ironworkers cried, and their bodies shook
as they stopped at his casket. His friends attended two funerals
that week, because another ironworker had been killed in the same
accident.

For many months after the funeral, my mind played tricks on
me. I could hear his voice when I was alone. I felt him touch me.
During the next couple of weeks, I lost fifteen pounds. I knew I
couldn't stay in Connecticut, because everywhere I turned there
was a reminder of our three years together. Our yard was filled

with animals we were raising, flowers we had planted, and stone walls we built together. Wally's truck and tractor sat parked in the driveway.

Six months after Wally's death, I thought I was losing my mind. I called my sister in Arizona and asked if I could visit her for a couple of weeks. She said, "Of course you can." So I flew out to Yuma. The Arizona sun warmed my cold body, and my heart began to heal. I would never forget Wally, but while I stayed in Arizona, I began to think a little more clearly, and the pain became bearable. Each time I saw a young couple with their arms around each other or one calling the other one "hon," my stomach would knot up, and I'd feel queasy. I began to resent intimacy between couples. I discovered several ways to work through or perhaps avoid grief, by staying real busy, shopping, trying to fix other people, becoming a martyr, or having a short romantic obsession. Grief sucked.

Just before it was time to fly back to Connecticut, I called my family and told them I had decided to move to Arizona. I said, "I'll pay the way for each of you to take a friend to Arizona, but if anyone doesn't like it out there, they'll have to pay their own way home." Then I sold our home and the farm equipment and called the slaughterhouse to come for the two beef cattle, thirty-six chickens, and four pigs.

My family and I loaded the cars, trucks, and trailers with our most precious belongings. With everything packed tightly, we opened the doors of our cars, climbed in, and backed down the driveway for the last time. My heart ached as I watched our home being blanketed with the beginning of a snowstorm, and I knew that before we crossed the Connecticut state line, the twenty-two acres we loved so much would be tucked under the storm's cover. We began our carefully planned three thousand-mile trip to Yuma, Arizona.

Our caravan consisted of eleven adults, a three-month-old grandchild, four cars, two trucks, two trailers, three motorcycles, and three dogs. The drive to Yuma took us seven days.

Under a blazing sun and amid hundreds of miles of nothing but sand, cactus, and tumbleweed, we pulled up to our new home in Yuma. I missed the forests, the green grass, and the cool nights, but mostly I missed Wally. But I had to forget Connecticut and continue the grieving process. I struggled through many months of emotional pain trying to accept his death. I was angry with my God for taking my husband and allowing me to have him for such a short time.

Six months after settling in Yuma—on a mid-July afternoon—the thermometer registered 114 degrees. My sister and I sat at a table in the Western Club, listening to western songs on the juke-box. The door opened and in walked a man in tight jeans, white shirt with sleeves rolled up to the elbows, and dusty cowboy boots. I learned later that all the men in Yuma wore cowboy boots, even if they weren't cowboys. Tony looked at me, and I looked at him. He flashed a lazy grin, slowly checked me out, and said, "New in town?" *My God*, I thought, *what a handsome guy.*

Tony Garza, a retired captain in the Marine Corps, talked from the corner of his mouth. He held me in his spell with his steely-black eyes. This couldn't be happening. Wally had died only a year ago, and this man was making my head spin. Tony worked as a car salesman at a dealership in Yuma. After a one-year courtship, he proposed to me, and I said yes. We married a year later, but it turned out the marriage was for the wrong reasons. He persuaded me to use Wally's insurance money to buy an older home and said we'd remodel it together. We spent an additional ten thousand dollars, and the house became a beautiful home. Then one day Tony came home from work with a handful of brochures and said, "Hey, babe, the company's going to Las Vegas this weekend for a new car show, and we can bring our wives. Would you like to go?" He spread the brochures of Vegas across the kitchen table.

"Wow!" I exclaimed. "I've never been to Las Vegas."

So at six o'clock on Friday morning, Tony spent a half hour stacking the luggage neatly in the trunk, and we headed for Vegas. When we reached the freeway, he patted my knee and said, "Are you excited?"

"Yes," I answered, not knowing what to expect.

"Have you ever gambled before?"

"Cards with my family...but that was years ago. I remember

they just sat around the table and got drunk and fought. When I was a little girl, I watched my dad read the newspapers, and when he found the page he was looking for, he traced the column down to the bottom of the page and found some numbers under 'Treasury Deposit.' Then he'd take out his old worn billfold and find a ticket with numbers on it, and he'd compare them to the ones in the newspaper. He told me it was illegal to gamble on the numbers, but everyone at his work bet on them, so it was okay.... I've been to some horse races, but I didn't like them."

"I can't believe you didn't like horse races."

"No, I thought they were boring. When we played card games, it was for nickels only. I played bingo a few times, but I didn't like that either. They were too slow, so I sat there and made fun of everyone. I'd call out 'BINGO' when only three numbers were called, or I'd take my dabber and cover all the numbers on the sheets in front of me. I sat next to a lady who spread fourteen lucky charms around her, and after she checked her twenty-seven cards, she glanced at my two cards and pointed out one number I missed."

"Yeah, I don't like bingo either," Tony added. "But I can't believe you're forty-nine years old and you've never been to Las Vegas! Do you know anything about Vegas?"

"Just what I've seen in the movies." And what I remembered from the movies was dancing girls and scantily clad waitresses delivering drinks to the men sitting around card tables. I sat in the darkness and quiet of the car with mixed emotions. I was excited to be going to Las Vegas but apprehensive about what Vegas would be like. I stole glances at Tony, but his eyes never left the road. I learned later that he only invited me to join him on this weekend trip because all the other salesmen brought their wives, and he felt obligated to invite me.

Hours later I couldn't believe my eyes. It was incredible! Twisting in my seat, I yelled, "Oh, my God!" Thousands of lights—blue, red, and yellow—rocketing around like popcorn, and all I could say was, "Ohhhhh" and "Ahhhhh...like the Fourth of July!" Tony grinned.

Tony parked the car, and we carried our suitcases across the parking lot to the casino. After checking into our room, we unpacked our luggage and rode the elevator down to the casino floor.

I heard the loud battering of coins against the steel trays echoing through the room. I saw card players sitting in circles around dozens of tables. Gamblers screamed and threw dice across a green felt-covered table, and a huge roulette wheel with colored numbers spun around. Hypnotized by the rotating wheel and the noise, I stood watching some gamblers pile plastic chips on their favorite color and shout out their numbers.

A woman jumping up and down broke my trance when she yelled, "I won! I won!" Several women sat next to her in front of a bank of quarter slot-machines scooping up their jackpots. I watched how easily they slipped their money into the machines, pulled the handles, and collected buckets of coins from their trays. I knew I wouldn't dare try the roulette wheel or a card game, but I thought I could figure out the slot machines.

The sign read, "FIVE CENTS." For three nickels, I could win a jackpot of two dollars and fifty cents…if the reels stopped at the triple bars. Perching on an empty stool, I scraped out a handful of change from the bottom of my purse. I thought I could afford to bet a couple of dollars. I held three nickels in my hand while I studied the instructions on the machine. It looked easy. The coins disappeared, and I pulled the handle and waited. Nothing. I read the directions again and deposited three more nickels. Aha! This time the machine stacked dozens of coins into the silver tub, and I grinned and said, "Wow! This is neat!"

When Tony came down from his meeting, he said, "How's it going, babe? You having fun?"

"Oh yes, it's great. I love it. I wish we could come here more often." He made no comment. He grinned slightly and turned and walked away.

I thought it odd that you couldn't tell whether it was night or day, because there were no windows or clocks anywhere. I played the nickel and dime machines all weekend and won more than thirty-five dollars. We attended the new car show and ate free dinners and buffets. On the way home I said, "I really hate to leave, but maybe we can come back again someday. I had fun this weekend." I leaned into Tony and asked again, "Do you think we can come back again someday?" He just gave me the old lopsided military grin.

A short time after we came home from the Vegas trip, we used the rest of the insurance money from Wally's death to purchase a used-car lot. We kept busy and never went back to the casinos. The marriage lasted only ten months when Tony asked me for a divorce. That afternoon I walked into our bedroom and grabbed the bottle of bourbon he kept on the bureau, and I drank for four weeks. That was after nineteen years without a drink. We divorced and went our separate ways, but I missed Tony.

I was alone, and I began drinking daily. I called Tony for help. I left a message on his answering machine, and about an hour later he called and said, "I'll come over and help you stop drinking, and I'll spend one last night with you."

A short time later he walked into the bedroom and locked the door. He planted himself between me and the door, crossed his arms, and grinned.

I started to shake and sweat. "Tony," I whispered, "could I have just one last drink so I don't get the DTs?" I knew I could die if that happened.

"No! You're done!" There was only one way out of the bedroom, and there was no arguing with Tony. He never hit me, but I knew I didn't stand a chance of leaving the room that night. The last thing I remember was lying on top of the blankets and my body jerking up and down. I knew I was having the DTs.

In the morning I asked, "Tony, how long did I shake last night."

"About four hours."

Totally exhausted, I asked, "Weren't you afraid that I might die? Did you know I could have?"

He spit out the words, "Well, you didn't." He turned and walked out of our home for the last time. Our wedding cake lasted longer than our marriage.

After years of abstinence, the progression of alcoholism was still there, and the hallucinations came back more vividly. The next few nights I tried to escape the shiny black snakes; I fought furry cats with inch-long claws and pushed bats and nasty bugs away from my face. I knew I needed medical attention.

5

Tommie and the Casino

Two weeks after Tony divorced me, Tommie came back into my life. I had met him two years earlier when I visited Yuma. When Tommie saw how sick I was, he arranged for me to be accepted into the LARC, a rehab house for alcoholics. I had stopped going to meetings when I moved to Yuma, because I was angry with God for taking Wally away from me. Tommie moved in with me, and I started attending meetings again. We enjoyed each other's company and traveled everywhere. We took my grandkids, Damian and Chelsea, to the Grand Canyon, the Petrified Forest, and other parks in Arizona. We flew back East, rented a car, and drove Damian and Chelsea through New England.

Another year passed with no more trips to the casinos, but in November of 1982, my bowling team was invited to participate in a national bowling tournament in Reno, Nevada. I began stashing my quarters in a drawer when I heard that we would spend the first night in Las Vegas.

The day of the Reno trip finally arrived, and six team members traveled in two cars to bowl in the nationals. After checking into a Vegas hotel, we all took off for the casinos. This time I wasn't nervous. With all the confidence I could muster, I pranced up to the nickel machines and dropped a few coins into the slot. Later I moved over to the dime machines and then tried the quarter slots. All the machines rewarded me generously. Lady Luck was with me, and my friends had to pry me away when it was time to leave.

The first night in Reno, there was no need to read the instructions on the slot machines. I was a pro now. Strangers shared their gambling tricks, and I discovered I had what gamblers called beginner's luck. Every machine I played, jackpots tumbled into the metal bowls. I had discovered America, and no one could take that thrill away from me.

I couldn't sleep that first night in Reno, so I got up at 4:30 in the morning and drove downtown. After parking my car, I hurried across the empty street, never giving a thought to the fact that I was alone in a strange town.

Once inside the casino door and before I could change my mind, I scooted over to the cashier and said, "I'd like one hundred silver dollars." One hundred silver dollars! I couldn't believe I was doing this.

He smiled and pushed the rack of silver toward me saying, "Good luck, lady."

My hands shook. I dropped the first three dollars into the machine, and while holding my breath, I slowly pulled the handle. God, I was scared! More than a hundred coins came rattling down in the metal bowl. I didn't know what I'd hit, but I kept plugging money into the coin slot, and the jackpots kept filling the trays. I was so excited, I thought I would throw up.

After an hour and a half, I drove back to the motel, still shaking. I had won more than five hundred dollars. I could quit my job and just gamble—shorter hours and better pay. Surely, something this much fun couldn't be harmful.

We bowled our scheduled games, and in between, we gambled. On the way home, I thought how lucky it was for me that Laughlin, located on the Nevada/Arizona border, was only a four-hour ride from Yuma. Maybe I was destined to become a professional gambler.

Tommie met me in the driveway when I got home and said, "Did you have a good time, babe? What's the big grin for?"

"Tommie! You'll never believe what happened in Reno! I went gambling and I won! Lots of money!"

"Really?" he asked.

"Yes, and we can drive up to Laughlin next weekend and gamble. Do you want to?"

"Yeah, I'd love to."

We spent the next weekend at the casino—and many more weekends over the following years. The first few months of Laughlin trips, I didn't realize we could spend the night there, so the drive home was a tiring ordeal. We'd gamble until four o'clock on Monday morning, and by then we were both too tired to drive home. Tommie would say, "Let me drive, babe. You must be tired."

"Okay," I would agree. "I'm pretty tired…and I've got to go to work as soon as we get back."

After about fifteen minutes of watching Tommie drive, I'd catch him dropping his head, and I'd yell, "Tommie, you're falling asleep!" So I always ended up driving home.

We made the trip to Laughlin twice a month for the next few months, and then it became a weekly trip. On the ride up there I'd say, "Tommie, let's watch a show this time or dance for an hour or so."

His answer was always, "Yeah, that'd be great." We always talked about it, but the closest we got to dancing was sitting at the machines next to the dance floor.

After the first year, I didn't care if I won or lost; I just wanted to gamble. I was having fun, and gambling relaxed me. Besides, it was my money, and I deserved a little break. I worked hard all week, and I wasn't hurting anyone. No one asked me for excuses, but I always offered them.

Tommie and I had a regular routine and always stopped to buy lottery tickets and snacks in Quartzite, a small town about thirty miles outside of Yuma. Our next stop was Needles, ten miles outside of Laughlin, where we'd fill the car with gas, use the restroom, and rush through the store, picking up snacks. I always bought the most recent copy of my horoscope to see if this would be my lucky weekend, and then we'd be on the road again.

Each weekend, I watched the other gamblers and thought that there must be a secret to beating these machines. Pulling the handle three times in a row and then pressing the button three times seemed pretty lucky, and it made sense—I thought. I tried counting to ten between dropping the coins and then counting to ten before pulling the handle. Sometimes I held my breath, and sometimes I closed my eyes. Or I'd play only the corner machines to start with and then switch to the ones in the middle of the rows. None of the systems worked all of the time, but they all worked some of the time. I just picked the wrong system most of the time.

One weekend when Tommie and I drove to Laughlin, we ran into a heavy rainstorm. It poured so hard that the wipers couldn't keep the windshield clear. When we reached Parker, which was halfway between Yuma and Laughlin, we saw signs posted in the road: DETOUR—ROAD WASHED OUT DUE TO HEAVY FLOODING.

Tommie turned to me and said, "What do you want to do, babe? Shall we turn around?"

Without skipping a beat, I blurted, "Heck no! We're almost there. Why should we turn back now?"

So after two extra hours of treacherous driving through detours and flooded areas, the car literally slid into the parking lot of the Colorado Belle at exactly 2:03 PM. At 2:04, I opened the car door, grabbed one suitcase, turned to Tommie, and said, "I'll meet you inside."

I splashed through the lake in the parking lot and dashed up the casino steps. Time was critical. Each minute wasted meant a minute lost at the machines.

We always stayed at the prettiest casino on the river, the Colorado Belle, which resembled a huge riverboat. After registering at the desk, Tommie and I walked to the elevator, and I pretended not to notice the banks of slot machines. I couldn't look at the machines, or I'd attack them. At 2:16 I unlocked the door to the room, and with one eye on my watch, I flung the few pieces of clothing from the suitcase onto the hangers, gave Tommie a kiss, and made a dash for the door.

After I spent a couple of hours at the Colorado Belle, I decided to wander over to the Flamingo Casino and won a one thousand-dollar jackpot. They presented me with a T-shirt with the casino's name in huge gold letters across the front. I waved it around like a flag when the cashier handed it to me. The T-shirt was a prize to commemorate my winning a one thousand-dollar jackpot. I neglected to tell everyone that I had lost six thousand to win the one thousand.

One weekend I made a promise to myself that I would control my gambling and use some willpower. I didn't want to stop gambling completely, just slow down a little. This show of discipline ended the minute I closed the door to our room and ran to the elevator to ride down to the casino floor. My heart pounded inside my sweater. God help anyone getting in my way…I would have trampled them.

I asked myself, why do I love this place so much? I felt a high like when I drank, but gambling was a high unlike alcohol. With gambling, I didn't pass out or act stupid. Well, I didn't think I acted stupid.

Once in a while Tommie didn't want to make the trip, so I'd go by myself. That was even better, because then he didn't keep asking me for money when he lost his. Sometimes when he'd come to me for more money, I'd hide from him. I told him every weekend to stop playing that stupid Keno game. Every time he came near me I started getting unlucky.

I soon began to keep secrets about my gambling, both the losses and the wins. If I lost at one casino, I'd go to the one next door and take out money from their ATMs, and then I'd run back and tell the people where I gambled that I just won a jackpot across the street. I told myself it wasn't lying, but it was tough trying to separate the lies from the truth. I solved the problem by telling myself it just wasn't anyone's business what I did.

After eighteen months of weekly trips to Laughlin, I realized my winnings weren't enough to support my casino trips. I needed more money. My credit cards were maxed out, and companies were sending me letters demanding payment. I had worked for the fertilizer company for more than four years and had a good rapport with John and his wife, Karen. If I needed more money, I could've asked them for a loan, but they probably wouldn't have understood if I told them I needed the money for gambling. They didn't gamble and did not approve of gamblers. I thought of inventing a phony excuse for borrowing money. I loved my job and the people I worked with, but I constantly thought about gambling. One afternoon while I sat at my desk planning my weekend trip, I thought about Keith, the boss's son. His job paid well, but he was always in a financial bind because of his drug problems. One year I handed him his W2, and he said, "Oh my God, did I really make that much?"

I answered, "Yes, you did."

"You know, most of that money went up my nose." And I remembered how often he had asked me to type up checks to "tide him over." He always told me he'd pay the money back, but he never did. After watching how he manipulated his finances, I thought about my problems and wondered if maybe I could "manipulate" some money, too.

So one Friday afternoon, alone in the office, I thought maybe I could write just *one* check to myself—just in case I needed some extra money at the casino. I told myself I wouldn't cash the check; I'd have it just in case. Keith had signed his dad's name on his checks, and maybe I could practice and do the same. After copying John's signature a dozen times, I slipped a check into the typewriter, made it out to myself, and carefully signed John Sloane's name to the bottom of the check.

I promised myself that Monday morning I'd void the check. It was just a loan, and the check was for only $287.54. I wouldn't cash the check unless I really needed it. But instead of waiting until I needed it, I immediately drove to the bank, cashed the check, and didn't pay it back the following Monday. But I would return the money when I won. And I knew I'd win.

My check writing continued. One day I had an argument with my daughter Beverly. We argued about her drug problem, and to support my side of the argument, I said to her, "Bev, you've got to stop doing drugs. I've been forging checks at work for extra money…just to support you and your two kids." She shared this information with her boyfriend, and the two of them, while on drugs, decided they should call my boss and confess for me. John's wife, Karen, worked with me in the office, and we had become good friends over the past four years.

A couple of days later, Karen approached me and said, "Marilyn, we got an anonymous call from someone, and the person said you've been stealing money from the company."

"Karen, that's terrible. Who called?"

"They didn't give a name, but when we called the police, I explained to the detective that there was no way you could be stealing money, because we never have any cash in the office."

"Oh Karen, thank you for trusting me." And then I added, "I think it's my daughter and her boyfriend that called. They're both doing drugs, and I threatened to kick her out." Karen believed me.

My deception allowed my addiction and my "borrowing" to continue. I couldn't bring myself to use the word "stealing," because I believed I'd pay the money back. My lying got worse, and I found myself playing mental games with Tommie. He'd call me Saturday morning at work and ask, "Babe, are we going to Laughlin this weekend?"

"I don't think we should," I'd answer. "We've got too much work to do around the yard."

"What's to be done, babe? I can do it all this morning if you tell me what to do."

"Well, we have to irrigate…and trim the bushes on the side of the yard."

"I've already done that."

I knew he had finished these jobs, but I still played mental gymnastics with him. "Well, wait till I get home, and we'll talk about it." I smiled as I slowly lay the receiver back in its cradle. I knew we would be driving to Laughlin, because I had reserved the room on Monday morning as soon as I sat down at my desk.

Tommie loved to gamble as much as I did, and at times he might have wondered where my gambling money came from, but he never asked. After all, it was my money, wasn't it? I deserved this weekend, didn't I? The more I gambled, the more money I needed, so I wrote more checks and gambled more.

After writing checks to myself for a year and a half, I decided one day to total up the amounts. They came close to four thousand dollars. I thought it wasn't really that bad, because with one big win, I could pay it back. No sweat! Because I was the office book-keeper and controlled the ledger entries, I could move the missing monies into different accounts, so no one would be suspicious. One month I'd deduct several hundreds of dollars from the inventory.

That created a problem, because I'd hear John lecturing the drivers: *"What in hell are you guys doing with the fertilizer? You've got to be giving this shit away!"*

The drivers looked at each other and just shook their heads. No one knew. So the next month I'd pad the vehicle repairs account. That wasn't much better, because again he shouted at the men: *"I'm going to have to fire the whole damn lot of you. Can't you take care of the damn trucks?"*

The gambling and the "borrowing" continued, and during my third year of driving to Laughlin, I decided to again figure out how much I needed to win to pay back all the money. Making sure no one was in the office, I opened the bottom drawer in my desk. From under some files, I pulled out a coded list of the check amounts. I had written them so they looked like phone numbers.

I plugged the amounts into the calculator and subtotaled it after I listed ten checks. I looked at the tape and was shocked. This had to be a mistake. The subtotal was close to eight thousand dollars, and I still had more numbers to add. When I finished, it came to more than twelve thousand dollars. I had been gambling for three years now. The following weekend, all I could think about was how much I needed to win to pay the company back. I walked across the casino floor and saw an old man in wrinkled clothes hovering over *my* machine. I waited patiently as he dropped in his last coin. If he thought I wanted the machine, he'd ask the change person for more silver, so I pretended to study the machine next to him. Everyone in the casino knew he was sitting in front of "my" machine. When he finally got up and walked away, I heaved a sigh. I tucked my rack of silver close to *my* machine so no one would come along and take my money. Someone told me that people steal money in casinos.

Looking around the machine, I made sure everything was in order. I shoved the dirty cups and ashtrays to the back, because I needed a clean space. While I plucked the gum wrapper out of the silver tray, I thought of the messes in my life with my family. I didn't need a mess around the machine, too. But I knew that in a few minutes, gambling would make all my problems go away.

I carefully twisted the straps of my purse around my knees,

so no one would take my gambling money. Now I could start to gamble, but this time I would gamble slowly. Taking a deep breath, I smiled at the lady sitting next to me as I reached for my tray of silver. "I feel really lucky tonight," I said.

She turned to me and said, "Oh, I don't know. I'm not doing so good."

"Well, I have a feeling that we're both going to win tonight."

"I sure hope so, or I'll have to go home broke, and my husband will be mad."

"He won't be mad when he sees you bringing home lots of money."

I stopped talking and tried to concentrate on my gambling. I *slowly* dropped the first three silver dollars into the slot and pulled the handle ever-so-gently. One blue seven on the first reel…another blue seven on the second reel…and then the third reel stopped and up popped the blue triple bars. Nothing this time, but I thought, it sure looked good. "Look at that, I almost got a win!"

Promising myself I wouldn't put more than one tray in each machine, I reached for another three coins. Each tray gave me thirty-three pulls on the handle. I was proud of myself. I had control tonight. This time the triple bar came up on the first reel, another triple bar on the second reel, and on the third reel, a blue seven. Still looking good I thought. All the blue sevens are right there. Taking another deep breath, I relaxed and casually looked around the room while reaching for three more dollars. I caressed *my* machine as I dropped in the coins, but instead of pulling the handle, I pressed the button. Three single bars lined up on the three reels. Twenty-five dollars. Ahead by fourteen dollars. Yes! I decided I better not talk to the little lady any more. I didn't want her to spoil my luck.

A half hour later I'd dropped three hundred dollars with no more wins. I'd forgotten my promise to put one rack in each machine. Oh well, the sevens will come back, so I'll buy just one more rack. You can't win if you don't play. I turned to the woman next to me and said, "I can't leave. I've put too much money in already. If I leave, someone will come along and win my jackpot. I have to stay here."

She smiled and said, "You're right!"

"I hate when someone wins at *my* machine or even sits on one of *my* stools. And I hate to see a person put in only one coin." She agreed. And again that night as I walked out of the casino—a loser—I looked around. I could always find one person in the casino who was worse off than me. I watched the sick alcoholic walking past my machine, and I knew he came only to finish the drinks left at the machines by the players. I wasn't that bad.

Four years after I started gambling, I sat at my desk at work and turned on the calculator. After plugging in all the figures, the amount of the "borrowed" checks totaled twenty-five thousand dollars. Some weekends I justified my check writing by saying if my boss were easier to get along with, I wouldn't be taking his money. It eased my conscience when I blamed someone else.

On the tenth of each month, the parent company in California sent a team of accountants to Yuma to audit our books. I knew they'd discover what I was doing on one of these visits, and I'd lose my job, my home, and everything I'd worked for. I might even go to prison. All because of gambling. What would my family think of me if they found out? I wished I could go back to my normal way of living and be a mother and grandmother. But, "I wish I may, I wish I might" didn't work for grown-ups, and there really wasn't a Santa Claus or a genie in a bottle.

Each time the auditors came, I didn't sleep for the three days they spent examining the books. I felt so vulnerable, thinking that at any minute someone might tap me on the shoulder and say, "Come with us." But they always left without finding anything. If only they'd catch me, this mess would stop. But they didn't. They audited the books each month for five years and found no money missing. The total had reached one hundred thousand dollars. I knew I should stop gambling, but I couldn't tell anyone, because they'd try to fix me, and I wasn't ready. I was getting ready to be ready.

Some nights when I sat in front of a slot machine, I fantasized about the big win, buckets overflowing with coins and racks of silver piled atop each other. In my fantasy I'd ask one the employees, "Could you wheel the money cart over to my machine, so I can load up my winnings?"

She'd answer, "Of course, Marilyn. You're having a fantastic night aren't you?"

And then I'd prance behind the cart, pushing it across the casino floor to the teller's booth while everyone in the room watched. I'd hand out generous tips to everyone who worked there.

But on my way to work the following Monday morning, reality would set in. I'd drive past the city library and see the homeless people, their belongings stuffed into grocery carts. I knew that one day I'd be pushing my cart along with them. I wondered if they'd accept me or would they judge me? What chain of events brought them to the library lawn? Did their first incident seem harmless, as mine did?

After years of shoving coins into the slot machines, I discovered I could take a row of silver from the rack, cup them in my hand, tip my hand over carefully, and drop three coins at a time. I could empty the whole rack in seven minutes, and I knew if I didn't hit a jackpot, I could lose eight hundred and sixty dollars in an hour. I plucked the coins out of the plastic cup by the handful, because I came here to gamble—and gamble I would. "You can't win if you don't play!" I thought, *how many times have I repeated that brilliant quote?*

Some nights when I walked up to the cashier's booth, I'd ask, "Which machine is hot tonight?"

One night the cashier pointed and said, "That one's ready."

"Why is that a good one?" I asked.

"A man just put twelve thousand dollars in it and didn't win anything."

"*Oh, I doubt that!* The jackpot's only two thousand!" I didn't believe her. "Why would he sit here and put all that into one machine?"

"He just got a million-dollar settlement from an accident, and he's on his way to Las Vegas."

I sat down at the machine and decided to add my three hundred dollars…put three silver dollars in, pull the handle, put three more in and hit the button…didn't work. Try two dollars, pull the handle; next time push the button. Pull the handle slower; yank it really hard. Stroke the machine and then curse it. Nothing worked that night, but I could wait. I prayed for *my* "lucky night." When I gambled, I found myself bargaining with God: "If you just let me win the big one, I'll quit and go to bed!" An hour later, I pleaded, "Just let me get even, and I'll quit." And then: "If you loved me, you'd let me win." Then I told him how to let me win. "I'll take the blue sevens or the triple bars or a couple of small jackpots."

Sometimes late at night I'd take chances running frantically from one casino to another behind the buildings in the alleys. Flying past the Dumpsters in the dark, I wondered what I'd do if someone jumped out from behind them. So I ran faster. Tucked between the two new eight-story casinos was a small, poorly lit casino filled with truck drivers and alcoholics. I thought this house might have looser machines. I ducked in the back door, but the room was so dark and smoky and crowded with rough-looking men, I quickly backed out the door and headed for the next casino.

I could only gamble on weekends, because Laughlin was so far away, so I made sure all the yard work and other duties around our home would be finished before Friday afternoon. On my way home from work that next Friday, the numbers on my odometer read 77,776.7 miles. Because the driveway to my house was circular, I could drive around until the odometer reached all 7s. With each trip around the yard, the odometer added one tenth of a mile. With my heart pounding, I raced around the circle, spinning gravel into the air while my grandkids waved from the front porch. When the odometer reached the magic number and rolled over to six sevens, I slammed on the brakes and ran into the house screaming, "*Tommie, come quick and see what happened. There's six sevens on the odometer—three for you and three for me.*" I twirled around the kitchen, yelling, "Let's hit the road! Right now!" Anything with seven in it was good luck—street signs, license plates, billboards, and even adding page numbers in a book. But this sign was special, because it had *six* of the lucky numbers.

As I drove down the streets in Yuma, I watched for cars with license plates with sevens in them, or if all the numbers in the license plate added up to a seven, it meant good luck. Or if there was a twenty-one in the number, I could divide it by three, and then I had three sevens. I believed in lucky jewelry, especially my crystals, and lucky clothes, like my red blouse. Sometimes I placed my hands a few inches from the machine and imagined I could feel a magical magnetic aura.

I worked diligently to perfect my gambling and become a winner. I bought books on gambling and tried everything I read in the books. In the casinos, I walked my route of machines and I would hit them, like a paperboy.

When it came time to leave the casino, Tommie wasn't always ready. I told him I needed to get home at a decent hour so I'd be at work on time. What I really meant was that I *had* to be at work on time, so no one would discover the forgery.

Ironically, the more checks I signed, the more responsibilities John gave me. Calculating the payroll for employees was one of my responsibilities, along with accurate accounting of the inventory and typing checks for the accounts payable. One day John came to me and said, "Here's the key to the gas pumps. I want you to control it. I think some of the drivers are stealing gas, and *if I ever catch him, I'll shoot the SOB.*" Now I had an opportunity to fill my car with gas before I took off for Laughlin. After all, he handed the keys to me.

I never figured out why I didn't have a nervous breakdown, because each week there would be another frightening experience. One Saturday after signing John's name to two checks, I stopped at one bank to cash one check, and then I drove to K-Mart to buy some things for our trip. When I got back in the car, I couldn't find the second check. I searched the floor of the car, emptied my purse, and checked the ground around the car. No check! I told myself to stay calm, but my heart started thumping. *Oh my God, what if I left it at work on my desk?*

I drove five miles back to the office, jumped out of the car, checked the office floor, and even opened the file cabinets. No check! It was Saturday, and since I was the last one to leave the office, no one could have found the check if I'd dropped it. So I retraced my steps, going back to the first bank and back to K-Mart. I checked the parking lot, and there in the middle of the lot, a giant sweeping machine made slow trips back and forth. What if the machine had vacuumed up the check? If it did, I'd be safe, but if it blew away before the machine reached it, someone would find the check. I decided I'd have to wait until Monday morning.

An hour later, Tommie and I made the trip to Laughlin, and I forgot about the check. I decided I'd just void it Monday morning. It always amazed me how the thought of gambling would erase all my problems.

That weekend I won six one-thousand dollar jackpots. I knew it wouldn't even make a dent in the amount I had "borrowed," but it was a start. I felt good. But then Tommie walked up. "Tommie, don't come near me when I'm playing. You bring me bad luck." I knew he was looking for some more money. "Why don't you play something besides that stupid Keno? Why don't you play the slot machines like me? At least I have a chance." But then we lost twice as much, so I chased him back to the Keno machine. By 3 PM Sunday afternoon, I had three hundred dollars left from my six thousand.

Monday morning the telephone rang, and Sandy, my coworker, answered it. I *knew* by the look on her face that it was about the check. She hung up the phone and looked at me. "Did you know you lost your paycheck over the weekend? Someone found it in the K-Mart parking lot and turned it in to their office. *How could you do that?* And how come you didn't say anything about it?"

Not only had I become a compulsive gambler, but I had also become a compulsive liar. I had the answer ready. "Well, I didn't say anything, because I knew when I told John I lost my paycheck, he'd just tell me to stop payment on the check and issue me another one."

Fortunately the office at K-Mart hadn't told Sandy the amount of the check, or they would have caught me. I had written the check for $832.79. Definitely not a week's salary. On my lunch hour, I drove to K-Mart and picked up the check, crossed the street, and deposited it into my account. My conscience had disappeared long ago. I remembered a Bible passage I read many years ago: "As a dog returns to its vomit, so a fool repeats his folly." And so I repeated my folly.

While I embezzled money, I carefully planned a system to

make the piles of canceled checks disappear. Memorizing the date the mailman delivered the bank statement, I made sure I picked up the mail myself and sorted through approximately three hundred checks, pulling out the forged ones. I listed the check numbers on a piece of paper in a code only I understood. I rolled up the forged checks, slipped a rubber band around them, and dropped them into my purse.

Once a week I referred to the list of checks I kept hidden in the bottom drawer of my desk. The numbers and amounts gave me the information I needed to help reconcile the bank statements. I wrote the numbers on the sheet so they didn't look like check numbers or dollar amounts. Instead of a number looking like check number 1784, I wrote it as $17.84, and then I copied the amounts to look like phone numbers. If anyone found my list, they wouldn't understand what it meant.

Some weekends Tommie and I took my grandkids with us. My family thought I took care of them, but I rarely saw them when I gambled. The only time I spent with them was in the restaurant or handing them rolls of quarters to spend in the arcade. While we ate dinner, a gal always stopped at the tables and sold Keno tickets. Tommy would buy Keno tickets for the kids, and the gal never mentioned it was illegal for kids to fill out the tickets. Maybe I didn't like Keno because the restaurants didn't have slot machines and I couldn't gamble while I ate. I never gave a thought to whether the casino might not be a healthy environment for the kids. Not only were they unhealthy for my grandkids but also for me, because I never ate or slept regularly. I sat for hours at the slot machines without getting up to go the bathroom or to get a drink of water. I never considered gambling as a problem; for me it was the solution to my problem. I wasn't as bad as the sick alcoholic who finished the drinks left by the machines.

Finding more money to gamble with in the casinos became easier each weekend. I used my credit cards and jokingly called it the "ATM card shuffle." I would take turns with several cards, and after midnight I ran the cards through the machine again. I had a plan where I'd go to a different casino and pull money from their

ATMs, so the other players and employees at my favorite casino wouldn't know I was losing. I needed to maintain my *image.* Lies invented themselves for me.

One night a woman watched me at the ATM, and I overheard her whisper to her husband, "Look at her. She's taking money out of the ATM machine to gamble with."

I whispered, "Why not? That's what the machines are for. This may be the three hundred that will win the big one." *Didn't she know that you need money if you want to gamble?* Sometimes the ATM didn't cooperate when I slid my card into the machine. The machine would spit it back out. A little message flashed across the screen: "Unable to perform transaction due to insufficient funds," or "Please contact your bank." I angrily shoved the card back into the machine as if to punish it. My God, how could they do this to me? This was my money, wasn't it? Walking across the floor to another ATM, I tried again. Same message: "Please contact your bank."

Sitting at the slot machine with my last twenty dollars, I complained to Lou, the man on the stool next to me. "You know what really ticks me off?"

"What?" Lou asked.

"When the ATM makes you wait until midnight before they'll give you more money."

"You know the casino cashes personal checks."

Surprised, I said, "No one ever told me that." I zipped over to the cashier's booth and asked the gal, "Can you cash a check for me?"

Without hesitating, she answered, "How much do you want to cash it for?"

"How much can I cash it for?"

"Well, we usually start with a one thousand dollar limit, and if you need more, we do a credit check with your bank."

"Oh, a thousand will be fine, but check with my bank to see if they'll increase that in the future." Just what I needed. I could play all night and never worry about money. I whispered, "Thank you, God."

I didn't really mind losing, but I hated it when *all* the money was gone. It meant I couldn't gamble any longer, and I hated the depressing feeling of being in a casino with no money. Gambling was the reason I drove four hours to Laughlin every weekend.

When I gambled, it was to get more money, and I always found myself with less. I gambled to meet new friends and hated everyone in the casino. All the reasons I gambled for were excuses and not reasons at all.

The Colorado Belle had a contest one year, and the prizes were three-foot tall, bright green Ninja Turtles. Every weekend for two months, Tommie and I crammed a dozen turtles into the trunk of our car—Michelangelo, Raphael, Leonardo, and Donatello. With each one thousand dollar jackpot, the casinos handed out a turtle, so all the kids in our neighborhood owned at least two sets of Ninja Turtles.

Somewhere in my gambling, I crossed the invisible line between "loving to gamble" and "having to gamble." Trying to escape pain or problems was a very isolating experience. One minute I'd feel lucky, and two minutes later I'd lose twenty tries in a row. A voice in my head screamed, *Stop! Walk away! You're losing, stupid!* But I couldn't walk away. The voice said, *This machine is going to pay off. Don't walk away. Someone will take your machine. You're due.* I was always on the verge of winning.

Sometimes at one o'clock in the morning, I'd slip into the lady's room and do my bookkeeping. Locking myself in a cubicle, I'd use my lap for a desk and add the amounts of the ATM withdrawals and the checks I'd cashed and then subtract the total from my checking account. This gave me an idea of the size of the jackpot I needed. I knew I couldn't be a compulsive gambler, because I only gambled on weekends. I didn't like card games or the race track, and the lottery and bingo bored me. I still had my home and a job, but I felt as if I were losing my mind. This was soon to change.

When my employer finally discovered my crime, the total amount I'd embezzled reached more than three hundred thousand dollars. The weekend before I was arrested, I came home with over forty-two hundred dollars, the most I ever brought home. On Monday morning I drove to the bank to deposit the money into my checking account, and I watched the gal behind the counter punch my information into the computer. A great big red spot flashed in the right-hand corner of the screen. She quickly turned the monitor around. "What's that?" I asked.

"I don't know," she said. Nausea rose in my throat as I watched her complete my transaction. She handed me my receipt, and I walked over to Ms. Peters, the woman who handled the safe deposit keys.

"I'd like to check my safe deposit drawer, please," I said, as I handed her my key.

She rose from her chair. "Certainly," she said. She returned with the bank's second key, and we walked to the vault. After she inserted both keys, she stepped back and said, "There you are. Call me when you're finished."

I prayed my legs wouldn't give out before I finished. Shaking, I carried the drawer into one of the cubicles and opened it. Everything was there—my small coin collection, some Indian jewelry, and insurance papers. Because I always carried a large purse, there was plenty of room to empty the contents of the drawer into it. I walked back to Ms. Peters and told her I had finished. She thanked me, and I headed for the door.

When I got to my car, I was ready to pass out. If the bright red warning on the computer screen was to notify the bank about me, I don't know why they didn't also prevent me from accessing my safe deposit box.

The last year I gambled and tried to "catch up," I had embezzled over one hundred thousand dollars in one year alone. After several hours of checking the numbers of dollars I had embezzled each year, I came up with these figures. The proof of the progression of the gambling addiction was on paper in front of me in black and white. My figures showed that the first year I wrote one check for 280 dollars, the second year the checks amounted to 2,720 dollars, third year 5,000, fourth year 10,000, and each year the amount doubled until the seventh year when the amount totaled 104,000. I can tell you how much money I lost to my addiction, but I can't give you a dollar amount on what I've lost in relationships, time, health, and other intangibles.

6

Life in the Yard

For sixty years, I took my freedom for granted. But now I could no longer walk out the front door and drive downtown to shop. Simple privileges were gone, like opening the refrigerator door to just check it out, sleeping late, calling someone on the phone to say "hi," or even trying to find a quiet corner to be alone. I missed my bed covered with pretty pillows, the pictures of my family on the bureau, and my bottle of Shalimar perfume. Losing all my personal effects was painful.

Instead, three inmates shared one closet where three pairs of jeans and three blue chambray shirts hung side by side. Each morning I pulled on the blue jeans and shirt, opened the front door, and saw 399 women walking across the yard dressed like me. Without the comforts of home, I would have to learn how to survive and adapt to my new surroundings. This would require tolerance and courage on my part because there was no place to hide in prison.

Rehabilitation at ACW did not include braiding leather key chains or making license plates. Instead, I struggled through a "learning to survive in prison" process. I read the GA literature my friends mailed to me, and I relied on the many self-motivating clichés that are used in twelve-step programs. If I felt threatened by another inmate, I would walk away repeating, "Easy does it." When the days seemed endless, I told myself, "One day at a time." While I lay on my cot worrying about my family and my future, I repeated,

"Let go and let God." As trivial as these slogans sounded, they gave me the strength I needed.

Warnings and regulations were posted on every wall. The inmates with sentences of five years or more conveyed their own set of rules regarding other inmates, especially the new women. I smiled at some of the women, but many of them were heavily medicated and looked right through me. The first time I said hello to a woman in the yard, she told me to mind my own business, so I avoided the other inmates when I could and silently repeated the "Serenity Prayer." Through years of listening and sharing at AA meetings, I had learned about the four parts of the "Serenity Prayer" from Jean S., my AA sponsor. She told me, "Each part of the prayer can be applied to a specific situation. The first part—'God grant me the serenity'—means you no longer hide from the past or live in jeopardy because of your behavior today, and you shouldn't worry about the unknown future. The second part—'accept the things I cannot change'—is to accept people, places, and things just as they are. We can't change others, and the only thing we can be sure of is how we respond to situations in our daily living."

Accepting the "things I cannot change" brought to mind a summer afternoon when the temperature in the yard reached 112 degrees. The guards and the inmates all walked slower, talked less, and stood in the shade. About 4:30 in the afternoon we lined up in the center of the yard and waited for the guard to announce, "The phones are now on." Instead, the guard's voice blared over the intercom, "There's been a problem with the phone system, and phone calls have been canceled." Everyone turned and stared at the intercom speakers, hoping the guard was joking. Some of the inmates burst into tears, while others stomped the ground. Knowing how badly I wanted to talk to my family, I took a deep breath and headed back to my room, reciting the second part of the "Serenity Prayer"—"accept the things I cannot change." Phone calls, letters, and visits from families were essential to the inmates' well-being.

"The third part," Jean said, "To—'change the things I can'— prompted me to analyze the issues around me. This meant not trying to change my family and friends and avoiding problems that were none of my business." Changing the world and others was not my responsibility, so I filled my free time by attending programs offered by the prison. I never missed any of my group meetings. These included AA, Seventh Step, Women Who Love Too Much, and Co-Dependency. I enrolled in DATA typing and computer classes, visited the psychologist and counselors, and changed the things I could.

Jean added, "And the fourth part—'the wisdom to know the difference'—would be knowing whether it's me or you that needs changing. We can usually determine who needs changing by listening to the signals around us."

"The wisdom to know the difference" required honesty on my part. In the past, I had distorted reality and had forgotten who or what needed changing. Now I needed to learn to differentiate between feeling and fact. I could easily reverse a situation or turn a minor incident into a Hollywood extravaganza. Or I might say, "If you hadn't done what you did, I wouldn't have to do what I did." It seemed easier to blame others and forget that I needed changing.

Many mornings when I walked across the yard, I could sense the tension between the women as the temperature rose above the 110-degree mark. The angry stares, the sly shoves, and the cursing under their breath increased as the day wore on. On those days, I finished breakfast quickly, hurried back to my room, and curled up with a couple of books. At the end of the day, I'd whisper, "Thank you God," and mark another X on my homemade calendar.

On the dining room wall, huge black letters stated, "No FOOD WILL BE TAKEN FROM THE DINING ROOM, and that means, not an apple or a crust of bread." To enforce this rule, an officer stood at the exit. One day I really wanted my apple but didn't have time to eat it. Sandra, one of my roommates, whispered, "Let me show you how we smuggle food back to our room."

With a quick glance at the guard, I said, "Sandra, I don't want to get in trouble. I'll get a write-up if I'm caught."

She whispered, "Put one arm across the front of your shirt, cover the apple with the other hand and slip it under your other arm down through the neck. Then grab it so it doesn't slide down when you walk."

It happened so quickly, I didn't have time to think. I expected the guard to throw me to the floor and put his boot on my neck while he shouted, "She's trying to smuggle food!" But he didn't. I realized later that what I did with the apple and how it made me feel was similar to the rush I got from gambling. Because I actually got a rush when I bit into the apple, I decided right there that I'd never do that again. It was like winning at the slot machine! I'd won an apple!

Each day in the prison yard was a learning experience. The constant changing of roommates by the prison staff brought serious personality clashes. The lack of privacy from both the guards and the inmates added more pressure to the strained population. Someone watched every move we made through windows with no curtains. Periodically, a guard's voice would blare out over the intercom, "Everyone to their rooms immediately!" They confined us to our rooms for no apparent reason, and we'd sit on our bunks and wait for the PA system to give us further instructions. Once we waited for two days to be cleared and were only allowed out of our rooms for meals. We were never told the reasons for lockdowns.

Even with the pressures from the system, several of the inmates acted according to the old saying, "Necessity is the mother of invention." I saw many examples. I watched a gal heat water for coffee by inserting the ends of two paper clips into an electrical outlet and then holding a cup of water under the opposite ends of the clips. It worked! Another ingenious invention was how the women used the irons. They'd go to the utility room and sign the iron out for an hour. Back in the rooms, they'd plug the iron in and toast a slice of bread on it. Tortillas were smuggled from the kitchen and heated on the irons as well.

One afternoon, while I sat on the grass waiting for Karen to come back, I heard a couple of guards sharing their yard stories. Officer Blanchard grinned and winked at Officer Graves. "Yeah," he said, "I've shone the light in her window every night for two weeks, and that bitch never wears underwear. I'm going to have to write her up if she doesn't comply with the rules." I wondered why the guard didn't write her up the first time he saw her butt instead of peeking through the window every night.

When the inmates stood in the mail lines and picked up their letters, they'd grab their mail and run back to their rooms to read in private. Many of the women talked about love, mainly the lack of it. Several gals came from families where the words "I love you" were never heard. These same inmates never received the letters they waited for. Fortunately, I received mail from my family and friends almost every day, and my family visited every weekend. The support of my family helped make my months in prison more bearable. When my daughters visited me, we sat at tables next to the guard's station. Each visitor could bring in a roll of quarters, and we bought sandwiches from the stand in the visitation area. My grandkids looked forward to playing on the swings and eating ice cream after lunch. Tyler would come running across the yard, holding his roll of quarters tightly in his little fist. He'd hand them to me with a big grin and tell me, "These are for ice cream...later." Then he'd make a dash toward the swing sets. He spent the hour working up a sweat, chasing the other kids. Damian and Chelsea were too grown-up to play on the swings. They asked many questions about prison life. I told them some stories about the other inmates and some of the reasons they had ended up in prison. I knew from my childhood that kids can accept almost any explanation about a situation but not knowing the answers confuses them. I wondered what Damian would think if I told him that Wendy was sentenced to prison for having sex with her eleven-year-old son. I didn't share that story with him.

After my family left each Sunday, I busied myself doing laundry. There were four irons, six brooms, and six mops for four hundred women. Because these items were considered weapons, strict records were kept on everything assigned to inmates.

One afternoon, while I stood in the laundry room folding my jeans, a couple of inmates were talking about "four-pointing" someone. When I got back to my room, I asked Karen, "What does four-pointing mean?"

She tucked a bookmark between the pages of her book and looked up at me. "That's when an inmate's a danger to herself, or others, or if she's been in a fight, and the guards have to physically take her down. They haul her off to the cells next to the guards' station. You can go up there and take a peek in the window, as long as you don't get caught."

"What happens to them up there?"

"Well, the guards take all her clothes off and strap her to the iron cot in the middle of the room."

My curiosity got the best of me. I grabbed a library book from my bedside table and tucked it under my arm. This would give me an excuse to be in that area if a guard questioned me. I walked past the guards who were busy checking the rooms on the opposite side of the complex. The isolation cells were on the north side of the guards' station, and as I walked down the narrow corridor, an eerie feeling came over me. On my left, I saw the three iron cell doors with small windows, three-quarters of the way up. If I stood on my tiptoes, I could take a quick peek. What I saw shocked me! The cell was windowless, but bright lights lit up every corner of the room. In the center of the room, I saw the cot bolted to the tiled floor. A thin plastic mattress lay on the cot, and thick leather straps with metal buckles hung from each corner. I sucked in my breath. The standard one-piece toilet and sink were attached to the back wall. There was no curtain around the toilet. The rest of the room was empty. Shaking my head, I hurried back to my room, knowing I would never forget that picture.

Back in the room I said, "Oh my God, that's awful. What's the strap at the head of the bed for?"

"If they're really thrashing around, the guards wrap that extra strap around her neck, and they call it five-point." She waited for me to ask another question and when I didn't, she added, "A couple years ago, an inmate broke her straps...pried a piece of tile from the floor and slashed her wrists. When the guards found her, they carried her to the infirmary, and the nurse stitched her up. After she quieted down, they brought her back to the cell and made her clean up the blood." This was a lot more than I needed to know. Karen was released the following week.

Most of the days in prison passed quietly. But one afternoon while I sat playing Scrabble with Fran, we heard loud banging and yelling coming from Judy and Carol's room. Carol came running out of their room screaming, blood streaming down her face. Judy had smashed a can of Rosarita's Refried Beans on the top of her head. Guards flew across the yard, grabbed the two inmates, and hauled them off to solitary confinement where they were four-pointed. I knew what happened in those cells.

With the severe punishments handed down by the staff, I was astonished at the risks the inmates took. Stealing from the yard store seemed to be a favorite pastime for some of the gals. When we waited in line to pick up our store orders, we stood in front of the counter, four at a time. The officer handed us our bags with our store lists. We then took all the items out of the bag, checked them against the list, and signed it if we agreed everything was there. Some of the gals discovered that they could lean forward when they signed their slip, and the gal next to them would slide a couple of items across the counter. The gal who had just finished the checklist would slip the items into her bag and walk out the door. Then the other gal would call the officer over and show him that a couple of items were missing. He would check her bag, and sure enough the items were missing and the store would replace them. When the store discovered what they were doing, we were only allowed to go into the store two at a time.

Occasionally we experienced a good day, and an upbeat atmosphere prevailed in the prison yard. On one such day, word spread among the inmates that the parole board would be arriving in five days. We waited anxiously for the office to post a list of names of women going before the board. When that day came, I stood in line with everyone else. I ran my finger down the list of thirty-six names and stopped at names beginning with L. There it was! Lancelot, Marilyn! I knew there wasn't a chance of my release, because I had only been at ACW for four months. The parole board met every six months so if I didn't make this board, I would be on the next list.

June 26 was the day of the hearings. The counselors gave us a scheduled time to report to the main office, and at 1 PM, ten inmates sat in folding chairs around the room. Each gal clutched her parole packet and waited for the guard to call her name.

Jessie Grant, a gray-haired woman who had served nine years for murder, sat down next to me. "I'm so nervous, I think I'm gonna puke," she whispered.

"I know what you mean," I answered. Jessie's name was before mine on the list, so when the guard called her, I knew I'd be next. I tried to remember the second line in the "Serenity Prayer"—"to accept the things I cannot change"—but it kept slipping away.

The guard came out and yelled, "Jessie Grant." Jessie followed the guard into the boardroom. I fidgeted in my chair until Officer Blanchard called me. I tiptoed into the room clutching my parole packet and tried to display a little confidence, but my knees shook and my mouth went dry.

Mr. Joe Tanner said, "So what do you have to say for yourself, Marilyn Lancelot?"

I had rehearsed my reasons for wanting early release. "I learned a valuable lesson, and I feel remorse for my crime," I answered, "and now I'm ready to go back to society and begin paying restitution to my victim." After I finished answering the questions, Mr. Tanner sent me back to my room and summoned my family. The guard told me the board would notify my family, and they would tell me the board's decision over the phone. But I peeked through the fence as my family walked to their car, and I saw the sad expressions on their faces. My daughter saw me and pointed to the ground. I knew the answer. Pretending it didn't matter, I smiled and waved to my family. Although I was disappointed, I knew I would be going before the board again in December, for my second hearing, and with luck, I could be released in time for Christmas.

The following six months seemed like an eternity. I went to work each morning, visited with Fran, exercised, and attended computer classes. And then it was Thanksgiving Day.

At 8:00 that morning, my daughter came to visit with two of my grandchildren. It was cold outside in the visitation area, and I only let them stay for one hour. Chelsea had shorts on, and goose pimples were popping out all over her legs. Tyler slipped and fell in some mud and got his new pants dirty. "Juannie, why don't you go home and finish getting your dinner ready?" I said.

"OK," she said, "but I hate to leave you here." She gave me a big hug and smiled. "I made some bread, and it turned out pretty good." Since I wouldn't be there to do my part, I had typed instructions two weeks earlier on how to prepare the turkey, stuffing, and gravy. Chelsea added with a grin, "I'm making the whipped cream and fruit salad." And then they walked away. Thanksgiving dinner at the prison was uneventful, and the food couldn't compare with our family dinners.

On December 6, I walked into the hearing room for the second board meeting. I was so nervous, my parole packet jumped out of my hand onto the table. My family sat quietly in the chairs behind me, and I gave them a quick smile. Ms. Agnes Buckley, a huge woman with menacing eyes, squared her shoulders as she turned the recorder on and nodded to Mr. Tanner.

Mr. Tanner tapped the table with his pencil and stared at me. With apparent disgust, he rattled off his first question. "What's a grandmother doing in prison?"

Swallowing hard, I answered, "I committed a crime, and the judge sentenced me to two years in prison."

He flipped quickly through my paperwork, not taking the time to read any of the words. "Why do you think you should be released?"

I took a deep breath and said, "Because I've taken all the programs and classes the judge and the counselors suggested, and I would like to be released to be with my family and start working to pay restitution to my victim." Taking another deep breath, I added, "I'm ready to become a productive citizen."

Mr. Tanner turned my packet over, cracked his knuckles, and without looking at me, he said, "Go back to your unit. We'll inform your family of our decision." Then the guard escorted me out of the room.

Again I made arrangements with Janet, the trustee in the lobby, to send someone outside and tell me the board's decision. She said, "Walk slow back to your unit, and I'll let you know the decision." I had only walked a couple of feet when she hollered out the door, "Marilyn, your family just came out. You didn't make it." In fifteen short minutes two board members, who knew nothing about me, had decided my fate for the next six months. It would be a wretched Christmas this year.

Of the thirty-six girls appearing before the board, twelve made it. Twenty-four would wait for the next parole meeting in six months. On the way back to my room, I talked to a couple of inmates who explained another option that I should check out. Jessie said, "I think you're eligible to get out early on TR to your PR or TR to your MR."

Totally bewildered and trying to act calm, I asked, "What in the world does all that mean?"

"Well, TR is a Temporary Release date to your PR which is Parole Release date and MR is your Mandatory Release date."

"I'm sorry. I still don't understand."

"Well, you could be eligible for a sixty-day early release to your MR date, which is May 15, 1992," Jessie explained.

"Really?"

"Yes. That means you could be released in March of '92, which is only three months away. Your counselor should have told you that."

Clutching my comp time sheet in my hand, I headed for Ms. Rawlins's office. The counselors usually didn't work on Fridays, but Ms. Rawlins had come to the yard to attend the parole hearings. On Mondays through Thursdays her hours were from 8 AM to 6 PM, and it was already 5:30. A line formed outside her office. I asked the inmate at the head of the line if she'd check with Ms. Rawlins to find out how late she'd be staying. She asked, and the answer was, "Late!" So I stood in line for another forty-five minutes.

Ms. Rawlins finally called me into her office and stood behind her desk pushing stacks of paper around and slamming drawers. Without looking at me, she asked, "What are you in here for, Lancelot?"

"Ms. Rawlins, can you explain my TR, PR, and MR to me?"

After taking a quick sip of her coffee, she said, "Well, according to your temporary and mandatory release dates, you're eligible for early release. That would be on March 15." With that, she slammed my folder shut.

Filled with frustration, I asked, "Wait a minute! What should my next step be?"

"You have to fill out your TR papers," she answered impatiently.

I was *not* about to leave her office until papers were in my hand. I lowered my voice and asked, "Can we do this now?"

Reaching again for her coffee, she saw that the Styrofoam container was empty. She crumpled it and tossed it into the wastebasket. "Well, we can fill them out right now."

"Great! Let's do it."

She opened her desk drawer and pulled out a new set of papers. She pointed to the places where I should sign, made copies, and handed me a set. As I was leaving her office, she added, "You'll be sent to New Dawn, a transitional house, and if New Dawn is filled, you'll probably be sent directly home by the fifteenth of March. Close the door on the way out and send the next inmate in."

"Thank you," I said, and ran from her office. I was relieved to hear the words *early release*, but angry that no one had told me this before.

The following months, I spent hours in the library to help the time pass quickly. The library had only one copy of each day's newspaper, and it was shared by four hundred inmates. One Sunday morning, I opened the paper and began reading an article about a "John Bulow, 57 years old, missing since December 5." He was last seen at a tire store on Camelback Road in Phoenix. Forty-five minutes after he left the tire store, his bank card was being used to make a cash withdrawal at a Valley National Bank. A short time later, witnesses saw Mr. Bulow's car heading west on the highway and said a man was signaling from the rear window, "in obvious distress." The witnesses noticed two people in the front seat. The car was last spotted seven miles east of Quartzite. Investigators "found a scene suggesting foul play" marked by blood in the sand and some of Mr. Bulow's personal items strewn about the area. Gas credit cards and bank cards showed travel over the next few days between Tucson, Blythe, San Diego, and Los Angeles.

There was a picture in the same article of a woman withdrawing money from an ATM; the bank camera had photographed her. The girl in the picture looked familiar. It was Karen White, my former roommate. Before her release, Karen told me of her plans to travel with her boyfriend on the back of a motorcycle, through the northern states. And today I read about her in the newspaper, missing and wanted.

Two days later, a small article on the second page of the paper read, "Accused of kidnapping and killing a man who has been missing." Two Phoenix people had been charged in LaPaz County with kidnapping, murder, armed robbery, theft, and possession of stolen credit cards. Both had been in separate jails on unrelated charges since the middle of December. Karen White, 36, was jailed in San Luis Obispo on a five-year warrant. Darrell Lee, 34, was in the Maricopa City Jail on an unrelated charge. Karen was expected to be extradited to Arizona sometime this week. I still have the little pill box Karen gave me on my birthday. The newspaper article shocked me, and it made me realize that if I didn't keep working my GA program while I was incarcerated, I could go back to my addiction.

Holidays were lonely times in prison. Inmates missed their families and the holiday dinners. Young mothers felt remorse, because they had no money to buy presents for their kids. Two days before Christmas, I walked to the mail room to check my mail, and there was a note in the window. "All Christmas decorations and little trees must be removed from all rooms and brought to the guards' office." Glancing around the office, I saw boxes of home-made decorations that the guards had confiscated a few days ago. The decorations were simple, but they added a bit of holiday spirit to the yard. On Christmas Eve, a half dozen inmates put their arms around each other and walked through the yard singing Christmas carols. Everyone opened their doors and joined in as the group moved down the sidewalks.

My family and my GA sponsors shipped me two boxes of canned goods, chips, salsa, and nonperishables. The prison bulletin stated, "All food sent to inmates for the holiday season must be consumed in a two-week period, or the guards will seize it." The two-week period ended, and I still had a can of salsa and a can of mushrooms. Knowing the guards would be doing a search, I decided to hide them. I dropped the cans into a plastic bag, tucked it inside my denim shirt, and headed for the computer room. In the far corner of the room, behind the line of computers, I found an empty wastebasket. Good hiding place! I thought. I dropped the bag into the basket and walked nonchalantly back to my room. I no sooner sat on my bed, when I got the "what ifs." What if someone decided to empty the basket tonight? I decided it might be better to move it to the laundry room. So I did. I played this game for an hour and ended up with the bag back in my room. I knew I'd get a write-up if the cans were found, so I opened them and shared the contents with my roommates. Christmas and New Year's just sort of drifted by.

January 11 was my one-year anniversary in Gamblers Anonymous, and my GA friends surprised me with a 4-foot-long happy anniversary card. Twenty-five of my GA friends had signed their names and written little notes. I borrowed some tape from my roommate and taped the card to the wall beside my bunk. I read it every day.

On February 4, I came home from work, and Mr. B, the yard supervisor, came running out of his office. He smiled and said, "Lancelot, pick up your green bag! You're going to New Dawn!"

For nine months I had waited to hear those powerful words! I took a deep breath and asked, "Are you sure?"

"Pretty sure," he said, "but it wouldn't hurt to check with your unit officer."

My friends screamed, "Yeaaaa! Marilyn's going to New Dawn!" New Dawn was a facility that offered the inmates a two-week period between prison and release where they would be taught how to survive without going back to their addictions or crimes.

I went to Officer Peg Darwin and said, "Is it true that I'm being transferred to New Dawn?"

"I haven't heard anything about you moving. But I'll check and see if it's true." Forty-five minutes later, an officer came to my room and yelled, "Lancelot! Go to the property room and pick up a green bag!"

I couldn't believe it. My heart pounded! I remembered all the women I had watched pack up and wait to be moved, only to find guards waiting at the gate to arrest them on a new charge. I ran to the property room, picked up my green bag, hugged Mr. B, and flew across the yard with my teeth chattering. I filled my green bag and carried my little TV. I kept my *GA Combo Book* with me to read while I waited. Later I met my friends for my last dinner at ACW and walked to my room to wait for the guard to call me.

The guard came back and said, "I'm sorry, but there's been a mistake. You have to unpack your green bag. And before packing it again, you have to write everything down on a property list." So I unpacked my things, wrote everything down, and repacked it. A custom in the yard when someone was transferred out was to give things away, so my friends came to my room and chose what they wanted.

An hour later, Officer Darwin called me into the unit office and told me to bring my list, my green bag, and my TV. She looked at my things, and with all the authority her badge and title gave her, she said, "Unpack them. We'll go over everything while I check them off your list."

Oh my God, I thought, this is making me crazy. To take my mind off the stupid repetition, I thought about what had brought me here and how my world had turned upside down because of my gambling addiction.

I felt apprehension about what would be waiting for me when I walked out of prison. When I gambled, I only gambled on the weekends and never thought that was a problem. How could I be a compulsive gambler if I didn't gamble every day? I couldn't have gambled every day, because I needed time to heal. And even though I didn't spend seven days a week in casinos, the thoughts of gambling occupied my mind during the weekdays.

After waiting another two hours, Officer Darwin came back to my room and told me to go up to the front office, get a 150-pound cart, push it back to our unit station, load my stuff, and then push the cart back to the main gate. Luckily for me, a few more girls also loaded up their property, and together we pushed the cart back to the lobby, unloaded it, and walked back to our rooms again.

Now it was time to call my daughters and tell them I was moving. The news sounded official. I stood in front of the pay phone and started to dial my daughter's number, but my mind went blank.

I couldn't remember either of my daughters' numbers. The harder I tried to remember, the more confused I got. I punched in every combination I could think of, but no luck. I either got a "Sorry this number has been disconnected," or a stranger answered, "There's no one here by that name." I hurried back to my room and looked for a number, but everything I had written numbers on was packed and locked up in the front office. Back to the phones to try again. This lasted forty-five agonizing minutes, and I was in tears. Then one of the numbers worked, and my grandson answered. *"Tyler! Is that you?"* I screamed.

My six-year-old grandson answered calmly, "Yes…Nana?"

"Oh, thank God! Let me talk to your mommy quick!" Juannie came to the phone, and I yelled into the phone, "Juannie! I'll be home in two weeks!" God bless her, neither one of us could talk. She gave me my other daughters' phone numbers, and I wrote them both down while we talked. Before we hung up, she told me that Graham was back in the hospital and not doing well. I prayed he wouldn't die while I was in prison.

Fran and I spent time together that night and made some plans. I said, "Fran, when we're both out of here, will you help me start a GA group for female gamblers?"

"You know I will."

"I remember how tough it was for the new women coming to meetings, and I want to make it easier for them. We don't want other women to go through what we're going through."

Fran nodded, "I'll probably be getting released a couple of weeks after you, and we can go to meetings together and talk about a women's group."

"And then someday one of us will come back to prison…to visit…and to start a group for the inmates."

"Sounds like a plan to me," she said, grinning from ear to ear.

I lay awake most of the night and wondered what New Dawn would be like, how long I'd be there, and what I would do when I got home. The next morning I didn't need the clock to wake me, because I only slept for an hour. At 4:30 AM six inmates met in the prison lobby and waited an hour to go through a body search. Then we piled into the prison van, and Officer Darwin drove us to

New Dawn, which was a huge, three-story building, situated on an acre of land in a residential area. An 8-foot block wall topped with razor-wire surrounded the facility. Our days at New Dawn were filled with classes on "how to cope after release." The counselors told us, "If you're in prison on embezzlement charges, you'll never have a checking or savings account, you can't buy anything expensive until you clear it with your probation officer, and you can't leave the city without permission. You'll never work in a position where you handle money or work in the accounting field."

After the first week of classes, the counselors gave us a chance to go shopping at K-Mart or Target, accompanied by a guard. After being locked up for ten months, the world had already changed. My first trip to the Target store left me feeling light-headed. I'd forgotten how many shampoos and toothpastes were stacked on the shelves. Hundreds of bottles and tubes for dry hair, oily, frizzy, straight, permed, and more, and in seventeen brands. And the toothpastes were similar.

Because I was still a prisoner, I felt like the word "felon" was tattooed on my forehead. I just knew everyone in the store was a detective, and they were watching *me*. Beads of perspiration covered me while I stood in the checkout line. I picked up my three dollars' worth of goodies and started toward the door. My legs stiffened, and I prayed the alarm wouldn't go off. The instructors at New Dawn had told us that if an officer confronted us, we'd have to identify ourselves as a felon.

During the two weeks at New Dawn, I started a list of things to do when I got home. At the top of the list was hug and kiss my family. The rest of the list included call my GA sponsor, attend a meeting, buy car insurance, have my glasses repaired, send some resumes to employment agencies, write to my brother in Connecticut, sign up for food stamps and the Arizona Health Care Cost Containment System, AHCCCS, go to the Social Security office, and call the probation office in Yuma.

It would have been wonderful if I could have added *seeing Tommie* to my list but that wasn't a possibility. We had lived together for many years. Every couple of years, he packed up his truck and moved to Florida, New York, or California for a few months but when he returned to Yuma, he always came back to my home and we began our lives together again. When I was sent to prison, the judge told us that Tommie and I could not have any contact with each other. I received a couple of letters from Tommie while I was incarcerated. After my release from prison, he visited me in my apartment a couple of times and I saw him about four weeks before he died. Our life together reminded me of the movie *Dr. Zhivago*, where Dr. Zhivago and his sweetheart, Lara, are separated for years at a time and the last time she sees him, she screams out his name as she sees him passing by in a trolley car. He doesn't hear her and the excitement causes her to have a fatal heart attack.

7

Release

The day finally arrived for my daughters to pick me up at New Dawn. I stood at the door watching for their car. When I saw them, I whispered, "*Thank you God.*" I hesitated as I stepped through the gate, eager to be released but remembering the many inmates who were arrested on some new count as they left the prison yard. My daughters and grandkids jumped out of the car, and we ran to each other and hugged and cried. It was wonderful to have the reassurance and security of my family! I turned and looked back at New Dawn and said aloud, "I won't be back." I promised myself I wouldn't dwell on the mistakes I'd made, but instead I'd remember what had happened, not with regret, but to see how far I'd come.

At last I was outside the barbed wire—without a guard watching me and without wearing handcuffs—for the first time in ten months. We sat around the kitchen table and talked late into the night. The next morning, I thought I'd lie on my soft mattress for an extra hour, but when the smell of coffee coming from the kitchen reached my bedroom, I jumped up and joined my daughters at the kitchen table. Kathy said, "Gee, Mom, it's so good to see you walk out of your bedroom. *It's been so long.*"

Juannie said, "It hasn't been the same without you here."

Bev added, "It's so good to have you home, Mom." And we cried and hugged again.

I picked up my first cup of home-brewed coffee. "Let's toast to a great year with lots of recovery," I said. After dressing in one of my favorite outfits, I went out to my car, which I hadn't driven for ten months, and turned the key. I drove downtown to check in with my parole officer and then to the probation office. They both gave me a list of dos and don'ts and you-better-nots. My next stop was the employment agency.

The nameplate on the reception desk read Binky Jansen. The perky blonde stopped filing her nails and reached back to sweep the hair from her neck. She gave me her best saccharin smile as she purred, "Hi there. Can we help you?"

"Yes, I'm looking for a job…and I have a resume."

"Great! Why don't you have a seat, and I'll tell Ms. Andrews you're here." A minute later she reappeared and said, "Follow me." She led me to Ms. Andrews's office.

Dressed in a light blue business suit, a striking woman of about thirty-five stepped around the desk and shook my hand. "I'm Carol Andrews, and welcome to Elite Employment," she said. "We can place you in one of the finest positions in the city."

"That's great," I answered. "After you read my resume, there's something I have to discuss with you."

She quickly looked at my papers and said, "Your experience is just what we're looking for. What did you need to discuss?"

Apparently she hadn't seen the word *yes* after the question, "Have you ever been convicted of a felony?"

Carol listened to my story about compulsive gambling and my theft to support my addiction. I couldn't believe it when she said, "I don't think your addiction would be a problem."

She stood behind the desk and handed me a slip of paper with an address scribbled on it. "I want you to drive over there this afternoon. I think this might be the position for you."

I took a deep breath and said, "Thank you so much."

As I walked past Binky's desk, I said good-bye. Without looking up, she said good-bye and continued filing her nails. I hurried out to my car and drove home to wait for my two o'clock appointment.

Little kids between four to ten years of age filled the building at 2240 West Butler Street. They were screaming, running back and forth, and knocking each other down. Mr. Arthur Lewis, the director, said, "The young children in our care center are mentally challenged, and you'll be chaperoning them in the classrooms and accompanying them on day trips. A bus drives them to parks in the afternoons, and it will be your responsibility to see that nothing goes wrong."

With confidence, I told him, "I'm very capable of handling children. I've raised five of my own."

He looked down at my resume again. With a slight hesitation, he added, "I notice on your application that uh, uh…"

I knew what he wanted to say, but I said, "Yes?" I could feel his discomfort.

"It says here that you have a…uh…"

"Felony?"

"Yes, what does that mean?"

So I related my story to him about the three hundred thousand dollars I had embezzled to support my gambling habit, but I told him I hadn't placed a bet in a year and a half.

"I don't believe this would be the right position for you," he said, "because when the kids go out on their day trips, they carry their lunches, and each one of them usually has between twenty-five and thirty-five cents in their boxes, and this may prove to be a temptation for you."

I knew explaining wouldn't help, so I took a deep breath and said as calmly as possible, "Thank you for taking the time to interview me and for being so honest." He shook my hand and wished me luck. I smiled as I walked to my car. He just didn't get it. I wondered how many people wouldn't get it.

The next day the phone rang. I picked it up, and Binky from the employment agency said, "Good morning, Marilyn. We have a job you can go out on this morning. Can you be there in forty-five minutes?"

Excited at the chance to prove myself, I answered, "Just tell me what the requirements are, and give me the address."

"It's a receptionist in a courthouse, and it will last for four days, and the address is 1501 West Washington Street. You can park in the lot across the street."

I quickly donned my black skirt and starched white blouse,

hopped in my car, and drove six miles to find the office building. After parking my car, I walked up thirty-six marble steps that led to a row of huge columns, and in the center of the columns, in huge gold lettering, I read the words, SUPREME COURT.

I walked around until I found Ms. Betty Paulson's office. She looked at my resume and smiled. "Welcome to our offices," she said. "Let me show you where you'll be working." She didn't mention the word felony. "You'll be sitting at the desk in the center of this corridor. You'll be the receptionist for the judges' chambers and the attorneys' offices." Uh-oh, I thought…something's wrong with this picture. "The buttons under the desk open the locked doors to all the offices and the chambers." As she turned to leave, she laid a piece of paper with a phone number on the desk and said, "You'll be responsible for opening these doors for the attorneys. If you have any problems, call me at this number."

Before she walked away, Ms. Paulson said, "I'll be back in two hours to take you downstairs to be fingerprinted."

I said, "Okay." I thought she must know about the felony, or I wouldn't be sitting here. I felt uneasy after being out of prison only four days to be sitting in the massive hallway in the courthouse.

After a couple of hours of answering the phone and opening doors for the attorneys, a female security guard walked to my desk and said they would be doing a clearance check on me. My heart skipped as we walked to the elevator. She explained that because of the high security in this building, a background check was mandatory. I had told the truth at the employment agency, but maybe Ms. Paulson hadn't been informed. While I sat talking to the investigator, I said to him, "You do know that I'm a felon, don't you?" Mr. Sanchez's mouth dropped, and Ms. Paulson covered her mouth with both hands. They quickly finished the meeting. Ms. Paulson told me to go back to my desk, and within twenty minutes, she stepped out of the elevator and walked across the corridor. "Marilyn," she said, "the gal whose place you're taking is feeling better, and she'll be back on the job in the morning. You can leave now, and we'll pay you for the whole day." I wiped the tears from my eyes as I walked down the front steps of the courthouse.

"Here I go again," I said quietly. After I got home and stopped crying, I called Ms. Paulson. "I was honest with you this morning and would you be honest with me?" I asked. "Did you tell me to leave because of the felony?"

"Yes," she said, "and I'm very sorry, but the position you were filling was in a very high-security area, and it wouldn't be appropriate for a person convicted of a felony to be sitting in front of the judge's chambers…controlling secured doors."

"Thank you for your honesty."

"Marilyn, if you can't find employment, because of *your* honesty, I'll help you find a job."

I never needed to call her, because I found a position the next day, but she'll never know how much she boosted my confidence.

When the counselors indoctrinated us at New Dawn, I remembered one of them saying, "The State of Arizona is an Equal Opportunity Employer, so if you have a problem finding employment, visit them." My next stop was the State Employment Agency. After filling out the paperwork for a temporary position, I drove home and waited. Someone called me that week, and I started working at an Arizona state office.

It didn't take long for my family and me to outgrow the house we lived in. Because I had a new job, I decided that I would look for a small apartment. I drove around looking at apartment complexes, but most of them were too expensive, and because I had no recent employment record, they turned me down. I eventually found a place that was reasonable, and if I could pay three months' rent in advance, they would lease it to me. I borrowed money from my son Gerry to pay the required rent.

The apartment measured 700 square feet and would fit in the living room of the house I lost through gambling. My son Graham was still very sick but he offered to help me move. I watched him as he carried the boxes from my car and thought about his gentle nature. I remembered his excitement when Tommie and Damian had found Ace on the canal bank and brought the puppy home. Ace ran over to Graham, and he patted the dog while reaching into the back pocket of his jeans. He pulled out a neatly folded red and white bandana and refolded it into a triangle while Ace sat and watched. Graham reached around the dog's neck with one corner of the bandana and tied it in a loose circle. Ace took off running back and forth through the orange grove. Graham loved animals and should have been a veterinarian.

Three weeks after I moved into my apartment, Graham called and said, "Mom, I'm back in the hospital again."

"Can I come and visit you? Do you need anything?"

"No, I don't want you to come here."

"Why?"

"Because you'll just preach to me about my drinking and drugs."

"I promise I won't say anything about that."

"No, please don't come."

And so I waited for another call from him. The hospital discharged him three days later, and he called me from his apartment. "Graham, can I bring you some food?" I asked.

"Yeah, and will you pick up my prescriptions…at Osco?"

"Of course. I'll be there as quick as I can." The druggist told me he could only fill two of the prescriptions, because AHCCCS wouldn't pay for the third one. The groceries came to twenty-four dollars, and I only had seven dollars in quarters and fifteen silver dollars, so I put some of the groceries back. I had no money to pay for the third prescription. Carrying his medicine and a small bag of groceries, I climbed the three flights of stairs to my son's apartment. I knocked on the door and heard him say, "Come in, Mom. I can't get up."

Graham had lost 35 to 40 pounds in three months since he had helped me move. I swallowed hard and choked back the tears. Black circles framed his eyes, and I could count every bone in his chest. His stomach was bloated. I knew if I cried, he'd ask me to leave. He whispered, "Ma, I think the hospital sent me home to die."

Crying all the way back to my apartment, I had no sooner unlocked my door, when the phone rang. I didn't recognize the voice. "I'm sorry," I said, "I can't hear you."

"Ma, can you come back and drive me to the hospital? I can't stop throwing up."

"Of course."

"But my door is locked…and I can't get out of bed. Stop at the office…get a key."

"Okay, I'm leaving."

"Maybe you better call an ambulance. You'll never get me down three flights of stairs…I can't walk."

"I'm calling right now," I said, as I ran for my car keys. "Juannie and I will be right there."

When we climbed the stairs to his apartment, the paramedics were already there trying to administer an IV, but they couldn't find his veins. Juannie and I waited while they loaded him onto a stretcher and carried him down the steps. We followed the ambulance to the hospital and stayed until eleven o'clock that night. Beverly, Damian, and Chelsea came to wait with us. We stood in a circle around the table in the emergency room, and he raised his head a couple of inches and looked at me. "Mom," he said, "am I *dying?*"

All I could say was, "Graham, we're all dying a little each day." I wanted to believe that at that minute my son didn't want to die, but I knew it was too late. We took turns trying to hold his hand or touch his shoulder, but each time we touched him, he said, "Please, don't touch me…it hurts so much." I felt his pain when our hands touched, but I thanked God that we all got a chance to give him a kiss and tell him how much we loved him. At 3:30 the next morning, the nurse at the hospital called Juannie and gave her the inevitable news. Graham found peace on September 6, 1992, six months after my release from prison. Juannie and I made the funeral arrangements for Graham and decided on cremation. I didn't dare tell the funeral director I had no money to bury him, but I remembered asking him what would be the least expensive funeral. The director told me that if we wanted to view the body, we would have to buy either a cardboard or a Styrofoam casket. I chose the Styrofoam, which cost us $2,400. I told the director I'd bring the money on the day of the funeral.

The morning of the funeral Gerry called me into the bedroom and said, "Mom, I know you don't have any money. Here's a thousand dollars toward the funeral."

I started to cry and hugged him. "Gerry, I didn't know what I was going to do today. I didn't know what I'd tell the man at the funeral parlor. He had told me if I didn't have the money, he'd have to send Graham to the county for burial." Graham's dad, my first husband, flew in from Florida and gave me another five hundred dollars. I made arrangements to pay the balance in installments. No one came to the funeral except family. Because of my gambling, I couldn't even afford a bouquet of flowers.

On September 14, I went back to work. It was a difficult day, but my coworkers were wonderful. They had taken up a collection for me, bought me a couple of plants, and gave me several cards. One of my coworkers wrote a very special phrase in the card: "May the sorrow and emptiness you feel be filled with the memories of the joy your son brought to your life. My thoughts and prayers are with you." The front of the card said, "Our deepest feelings can't always find their way from hearts to words." I truly appreciated the prayers and concern for my son and my family. Without all the support, it would have been much more difficult.

A few weeks after the funeral, my family and I walked to the top of a small desert mountain and threw Graham's ashes into the wind. We laughed when the wind wouldn't cooperate, and the ashes came back down and clung to our clothing and our hair. We managed to smile and turned our eyes toward the heavens. For months after Graham's funeral, I noticed young men walking on the city sidewalks, standing at a bus stop, or in line at the grocery store. So many of them looked like my son.

Two months before Graham died I had enrolled in a community college. My first day of school started three days after his funeral. I wanted to cancel my class, but if I didn't attend, I would have lost the Pell Grant the state awarded me. For forty-five years I had dreamed of going to college, and I wanted to fulfill that dream. I attended a two-year college without missing a day or being late, and I worked full-time.

In March of the following year I filed tax forms with adjusted income to include the embezzled funds. The IRS calculated the taxes due, which included late charges, penalties, and failure to include all income penalties and several other fees. The total came to over 175 thousand dollars. The IRS placed a levy on my checking account and took the 210 dollars I had saved to pay my rent. I never tried to evade taxes, and I responded to every letter the IRS sent me.

A friend helped me set up an appointment with the tax bureau, and the following Monday I walked into the IRS building in downtown Phoenix and waited in line to be called. Sam Carson, the man at the window, politely asked, "What can we do for you today?"

"Well," I said, "I'm here to see if you can write a release for the levy on my payroll check. I can't live on what's left if you do this to me."

"Well, you can fill out the necessary paperwork, and we'll take a look at it."

"I just told you I can't live on what's left if you do this."

"Like I said, fill out the necessary paperwork. A decision like this has to come from our office in Utah."

"You have to do this now," I pleaded. "Can't you call someone and get permission? I'm not leaving here until you do. I'm either going to throw up all over your desk or kill myself right here in front of you!"

"Calm down! Let me see what I can do." Shocked at what I'd just said, I wondered what I'd do if he went into the back room and called the police and they came and arrested me. Mr. Carson came back in about twenty minutes and smiled when he handed me a paper. "Here's the release for the levy on your payroll check. If you take it to your payroll department, they'll remove it."

"Thank you so very much," I said. "You don't know what this means to me." I left and headed for the payroll department.

Three weeks later, the IRS put another levy on my checking account and took two hundred dollars I had saved to pay some bills. I headed back to the IRS office and began the argument again.

Having to cope with Graham's death, the IRS, and school, I became really stressed. I had been attending college for eight months now. And then my daughter Beverly and my two grandchildren moved in with me after being evicted from their apartment. She also brought three dogs. I don't know how we managed in that tiny apartment.

One year after Graham died, Tommie's son, Mario, called us and told us his dad had died from a massive heart attack. It was another sad day for our family. Tommie had been such a huge part of our lives for seventeen years. We had formed a heartfelt relationship when I first visited Yuma. We parted many times— Tommie moved away, I remarried and divorced, he remarried and visited me often—and we always drifted back together. Tommie taught our family a different set of values and priorities. He respected nature and the desert and changed my way of thinking about life, from constantly worrying about everything to relaxing and "smelling the roses."

I set the clock before I went to bed that night, so we wouldn't be late for Tommie's funeral. When the alarm rang, I turned over and grabbed the clock and pressed the off button. Time is important to me today, but I remember ten years ago, time was measured by trips to the casinos in Laughlin, lies I told about money, and the manipulations to cover my gambling addiction. But I was home now, and when I held the clock in my hand, my fingers traced a rough area on the back of it. I knew what it was without looking. The number 85235 had been engraved on the back. My radio and my hair dryer had the same number. It was my prison number.

Our family drove to Tucson for the funeral. After the services, we were driving back to Phoenix and Damian turned to me and said, "Nana, when the priest was talking, there was a ray of sun coming down through the stained glass window of Saint Thomas…and light was shining right on your head. There was only one ray of sun in the whole church."

Bev added, "I saw it too."

"That's Tommie, smiling down on us," I said.

"I got the *chills* when I saw it," Damian said.

On our way home I thought about the deaths of loved ones in the last few years. The loss of my parents, Wally, Graham, and Tommie had devastated me. I learned through their deaths that grief does not have to be gotten over as quickly as possible or privately. Everyone should grieve in his or her own way, and there's no right or wrong way. Time alone will not heal us, but time will lessen the degree of the pain. Only grieving can heal grief, and it takes as long as it takes. Everyone is different.

Six weeks after Tommie's funeral I called Beverly into my room and said we needed to talk. I said, "Bev, I need to live alone again. I feel like a prisoner in my bedroom in my own apartment."

"I know," she said. "You told me when I moved in that I could stay here for six months, eight months, or ten months, or however long it took to save some money."

"Bev, I'm having a problem trying to stay out of my grandkids' lives. Damian's been kicked out of school, arrested for possession of marijuana, and stays out all night. Some nights I lay awake half the night wondering where he is…maybe it's better I don't know."

"I know it's tough on you, Mom, but I *am* trying. I'll start looking for an apartment." I decided to give her some more time.

The next five or six years were uneventful. My life consisted of going to work, attending GA meetings, and helping other compulsive gamblers. I had worked for the state for more than five years and I felt like a permanent fixture in my department.

The Monday morning after my talk with Bev, I unlocked the front door to the office, switched on the light by the receptionist's desk, and moved the button next to my name over to the *IN* position. Pictures of my grandkids, pretty plants, and knickknacks decorated the shelves in my cozy cubicle. Two years earlier, Bob Hansen, my boss, moved me to a desk by the window. Our offices were on the eighth floor and I loved watching the traffic moving along Central Row.

I walked to my desk, put my purse in the bottom drawer, switched on the radio and the computer at the same time, and was ready to work. I checked the mail on my desk leftover from Friday and felt someone behind me. I turned and saw my boss. Smiling, I said, "Good morning, Bob. Did you have a nice weekend?" I had worked as Bob's administrative assistant for five years. I knew his family, and we worked well together. We were both Geminis, and our twins were compatible. Everyone in the office knew of Bob's hobby of rock collecting, and he loved talking about his desert trips.

When Bob said, "Come into my office. I want to talk to you," my first thought was that he must have been out rock hunting and wanted to show me what he had found.

Following Bob into his office, I smiled as I slid into one of the red chairs at the end of his desk. I watered the plants in his office each week, and this morning they looked healthy and green. I loved my job, and I loved working for Bob. I looked at the top of his desk and didn't see any new rocks. Then I heard the office door quietly close. Uh-oh, Bob never closed his office door to show me rocks. My heart sank! Oh, my God, something's wrong. Maybe something was missing in the office, and I was the prime suspect because of my past.

He walked around to the back of his desk, grabbed the arms of his chair, and as he sank into the cushion, he said, "Marilyn, Dr. Alvarez found out about what you did." Dr. Martha Alvarez was the director of our department, and everyone jumped when she spoke. My head started spinning, and I felt nauseous. I couldn't talk. I couldn't even think. Why did he say that? What did they know, and what did they think I had done?

Bob waited a couple of minutes, straightened his tie, and said again, "Dr. Alvarez and some of the supervisors are worried about your working here."

"I don't understand. What are they worried about?"

"Well, it says on your application that you were convicted of a felony."

"Oh, my God! Why after five-and-a-half years are you asking me these questions? Why didn't you ask me when you hired me?" Would I be fired? What was going to happen? My stomach began to cramp, and I thought of the jobs I had interviewed for six years ago and had been turned down because of the word *felon* on my application. And here it was again. I took a deep breath and sat up straight in the red chair. "I didn't lie on my application," I murmured. "I wrote down *felon* like I was supposed to do."

"Well, the supervisors and Dr. Alvarez are worried, because you're a felon, and you handle all this money for the department," Bob said. "You're receipting between seven hundred thousand and nine hundred thousand dollars each year, and you committed a crime."

I looked around the office but couldn't find anything to focus on. Confused and afraid, I glanced at Bob again. Swallowing hard, I whispered, "Bob, I am probably one of your *most honest* employees, because I've been on probation for five years and have two more years to go. If I commit another crime, it's back to the Women's Prison for me. And you can share this with the supervisors and Dr. Alvarez. I don't want to go back to prison."

"I'm sorry, Marilyn."

"Can you change my job description and assign another employee to take care of the deposits?" I had showered that morning, but suddenly I felt unclean. My life was messed up again, and I knew my crime would haunt me till the day I died. I forged those checks because I needed money for gambling, but I no longer gambled. No one would understand, and I didn't understand why they didn't understand. Why didn't they look at my application five years ago? Why had they waited so long?

I think Bob could see how frightened I was, or perhaps he could feel my panic bouncing off the walls. He looked at me and said, "I'll talk to the supervisors and try to explain what you just told me, but I think Dr. Alvarez wants to talk to you."

I met with Dr. Alvarez and she thanked me for my honesty, commended me for turning my life around, and apologized for no one addressing the problem at the time of my hire. She also assured me that my job performance was exemplary and there would be no problem with my continuing in my administrative position. *How many years would my past continue to cause problems.*

Several days later my probation officer called and said I was delinquent in my restitution payments and threatened to put me back in prison. Weary from fighting the system and filled with anger I said, "Go ahead. Send me back to prison. I wouldn't mind for a minute! At least in prison no one bothered me about making payments to anything. No light bill, water bill, no rent payments—go ahead and send me back," I shouted.

"No, we don't want to send you back to prison," he replied. "Why don't you send us an updated income statement, and we'll see if the judge can adjust your payment plan?"

I sent him the statement, and the judge temporarily lowered

the payments until I could afford to send the one hundred dollars each month.

Six years after my release from prison, my son Gerry and his wife invited the family to spend Christmas Day at their new home. We sat around the Christmas tree watching the grandkids open their presents, and Gerry came over to me and said, "Mom, come to the bedroom. I have something for you." In the room he turned to me. "Open your hand." He dropped something into it and closed my hand. When I opened my fingers, I saw a beautiful gold pendant in the shape of praying hands.

"Oh, Gerry!" I squealed, "I used to have a pendant just like this! But I lost it about eight years ago."

"Yes, I know…these are yours."

"Where did you get them?"

"I took them from your jewelry box eight years ago. I was going to sell them to buy beer, but I couldn't when I saw what they were. My conscience bothered me, and then I had them for such a long time, I couldn't give them back to you. I was too embarrassed."

"Gerry, I love you and thank you for not selling them. And thank you for giving them back. They're very dear to me. Lee, my friend in AA, gave them to me fifteen years ago."

When I attended the next GA meeting and told this story to the group, tears filled the eyes around the table. I smiled and said, "I'll have to go buy a gold chain so I don't lose it again."

Sarah, the gal sitting next to me, reached her hands behind her neck and unfastened her gold chain. "Here's a chain for you to hang the praying hands on. It's gold, and I have another one at home."

"Oh, no! I can't take your chain."

Everyone around the table said practically in unison, "Sarah wants to give you a gift, and you should take it and say thank you!"

I put my arms around her and said, "*Thank you, Sarah…I love you.*" I glanced around the table and saw everyone dabbing at their eyes while Sarah threaded her chain through the praying hands and slipped the necklace around my neck.

8

Female Gamblers

The women in the Arizona Gamblers Anonymous Groups were a close-knit bunch. Years ago, when I attended my first meetings and met another female gambler (Lynne from California), it made such a positive impact on me. What could I have done for the other women who came to one or two meetings fifteen years ago and never returned? Would it have been easier for them to identify with the gamblers' feelings if they had met another female? I had vowed that if I got a prison sentence, I would start a women's GA group after my release. I would share the hope and strength that Lynne had shared with me and show these women how they could stop gambling and begin a new way of life. Through the years, Lynne and I formed a beautiful friendship. She was and has been instrumental in my recovery, and I'm grateful to call her my friend and GA sister.

The first Gamblers Anonymous meeting in Arizona was in April 1973, and for the first twenty years, a small number of women walked through the doors—and left. By their own admission, the men didn't quite know what to do with them and couldn't understand how anyone who played bingo, slot machines, and scratch tickets could possibly create problems in their lives. Some of the comments I heard during my first few months in the program were:

"You haven't gambled long enough."

"You haven't lost enough to be a *real* gambler."

"I've tipped a cocktail waitress more than you've lost in your whole gambling career!"

"You don't play *real* games."

Too often the women's tears and stories were ridiculed. They were hit on by the men with comments like, "Let's go for coffee… at my place, baby," or "You need someone who understands you."

The women didn't stay, and the men scratched their heads and muttered, "Women just don't seem to have what it takes to stay in recovery."

When I attended my first GA meeting, I stayed because I knew twelve-step programs worked, and I was determined to stop gambling. I could not and would not be chased away, but I saw many who were.

My vow to start a women's meeting in Phoenix was fulfilled a couple of months after my release from prison. I knew women needed a place to feel safe and a place where their issues could be validated and freely felt. A women's group would give us the opportunity to comfortably discuss issues unique to women's life experiences. We could feel more relaxed with other women and would be able to examine our guilt, our powerlessness, and our responsibilities in matters that pertained to women. Some of our members had low self-esteem and often failed to give credit where credit was due—to themselves. The meeting would help the women understand how and why they gambled and would provide a safe place where tears could flow. And no one would be more interested in her body than her therapy.

Three months after my release from prison, three women came to my apartment for the first "Women Only" GA meeting on June 19, 1992. To my knowledge, our "Women Only" GA group was the first women's group that met weekly anywhere in the world. I thought, if AA could have a Women's Only group, why couldn't GA? In the beginning the meeting struggled, but the women persisted. A few nights that first year I sat alone with my coffeepot. Some nights it would be just Fran and I, and we would read from the *Combo Book* for twenty minutes and then eat potato chips and play Scrabble. As the months passed, the women's meeting outgrew my apartment, and we moved to Fran's home, then to Sally's, and then Debbie's. Two years later, we could afford to rent a room in a church.

At our initial meeting of the Women's Group, the topic for discussion was "What are our expectations of the Women's Group?" Since that time, some of the most popular topics have been: how we handle pressure; have our values changed or just our attitudes; spirituality; the dream world; consequences of our gambling; unwillingness to accept reality; character changes; choices today; serenity; willingness; abstinence versus recovery; gratitude; guilt; and feelings.

Some of the men in the area were upset when we started a group for women. They told us they were coming by to crash our meeting. The main office of Gamblers Anonymous in Los Angeles said they wouldn't recognize or list our meeting in the directory because it was for "Women Only." We told them that we were going to continue to meet, and if necessary, we would change our name to "Female Gamblers in Recovery."

The meetings now average twenty to thirty attendees, and the largest meeting we've had was at our tenth anniversary where we also invited the men. That night sixty members came to celebrate. We always encouraged members to attend other meetings in the valley, not only the women's group. By attending the mixed groups, the women found new strength and courage, and the men gained a new understanding of women and became more humble and accepting. But the women kept their women's room for issues many felt could not be shared in mixed rooms.

We discovered that not all women have the same goals as men, and that our definition of success was not the same as the men's definition. We also found that we gambled for different reasons than our male counterparts. Our reason was to escape, and the men's was usually for power.

Shortly after we moved into the church, we introduced the Step Study meetings. They began in January, and we spent four weeks on each step. Years later when I checked past attendance books, I was pleased to see that the members who had attended the step meetings were still in recovery.

Meanwhile, one of the men who answered the GA hotline,

Don H., agreed that most women *did* gamble differently than men; that their personalities were different than those of the guys in the room; and that maybe the women should talk to other women who understood. He referred women to women and continues to do so to this day. I have recently looked at the list of Gamblers Anonymous Meetings on the Internet and noticed that there are several women's meetings around the country and they are listed as "women preferred."

One Friday night a woman walked into our meeting and through tears shared a painful story. She had gambled after she promised her husband she would never gamble again. When she told him about it, he became angry. "You know what you have to do now," he said. "You promised you'd never gamble again." He walked over to where she stood and unzipped his pants, while she got down on her knees in front of him. We told her that she would never have to do that again. This was a story that could not be shared in a mixed group.

Today, Phoenix and the surrounding area have more than thirty GA meetings each week. Of these, two are women's meetings, and women make up more than 45 percent of the GA fellowship. Most men now agree that women have brought spirituality and the talk of recovery to the rooms.

Referring women to women and encouraging women's meetings has its place, and it's an important place. The Phoenix women's group celebrated its fourteenth year of continuous weekly meetings in June 2006. All women may not identify with a women's group or feel the need for one—and that's okay. We explain to these women that there are some women who don't feel comfortable sharing some issues in front of men and feel more at ease discussing personal problems in a "women's only" group. The women who do *not* need such a meeting may be the very women who could lead a meeting and help women who benefit from starting their recovery in a more protected environment.

I discovered that when I sat in the women's group, I couldn't use my wiles with the other females like I could with the men. A woman can't con another woman, so sharing at women's groups caused me to look at myself more honestly.

Two elements are needed for success: women who are committed to helping heal other women and men who will support them and refer women to women. When I am invited to speak on the topic of women at conferences, I always ask this question: "If there's a man in this room who has said at one time in his life, 'I don't understand women,' will you please raise your hand." There's always a sea of waving hands in the audience. Women are different—emotionally, physically, mentally, and spiritually. And men *don't* understand everything about us. That's why women's groups are necessary.

Let me invite you to a typical women's meeting. It was a Friday night in August, one of those humid days when the air hung heavy. Feeling tired and not wanting to leave my air-conditioned apartment, I pulled myself up the twenty-seven cement steps to the Friday night women's meeting. Sometimes the air conditioner didn't work, and if this was one of those nights, I knew the room would be miserable. The temperature in Phoenix had reached 112 degrees that day. For five years I had faithfully attended the women's meetings, and tonight I hoped a newcomer might show up—then I'd be glad I'd come. I opened the door and smiled. Not only was it cool, but in the far corner of the room I saw two newcomers hiding behind their purses. With a big grin on my face, I walked across the room and put out my hand. "Hi, my name is Marilyn L. Is this your first meeting?"

One gal answered, "Yes. I'm Shirley, and this is my first meeting, but I'm not sure I should even be here."

The other gal hesitated, slowly reached her hand out to meet mine, and said, "I'm Janet. I know I should be here. I'm in a lot of trouble. I feel just terrible." And she began to cry.

"Janet and Shirley, you're in the right place. If you think you have a gambling problem, we can help you. Not many women walk through that door and tell us that their life is great, but now they want to stop gambling. All the women you'll meet tonight came here because of gambling problems." They both nodded. "We'll show you how we stopped gambling," I continued, "and how Gamblers Anonymous can turn your life around. Would you like a cup of coffee while we're waiting for the meeting to start? You don't have to be nervous. No one here will judge you." I handed them each a cup. "We all walked through that door just like you did tonight, and we all cried."

The three of us sat and talked while we watched the members fill the chairs around the table. Ten minutes later Barbara L., the chairperson, called the meeting to order. She introduced the two new women to the group, and we welcomed them. Seventeen members attended the meeting that night, including the two new people. Everyone in the room took turns reading out of the *Combo Book*. Barbara announced the upcoming birthdays and GA events and then suggested a topic for the meeting. Because of the two new people in the room, she suggested we discuss what had brought us here and how we were coping with problems in our lives today.

It occurred to me that we always discussed this topic when we had new people. Nevertheless, I was grateful for the subject, because I never wanted to forget why I needed to keep attending meetings. Then Barbara announced, "The floor is open for anyone to share."

Sylvia, a tall gal with a long blond ponytail, raised her hand. "My name is Sylvia T., and I'm a compulsive gambler. I haven't gambled for seven weeks. I didn't think I had a gambling problem. I thought if my husband were nicer to me, I wouldn't need to gamble. But even when he started being nice to me, I still gambled. Then I started lying and stealing the grocery money for trips to the casinos. After spending a night in front of a slot machine, I came home about three o'clock in the morning, and my husband and my kids were sitting in the living room waiting for me. My heart pounded when I saw the bank statements in one of Bill's hands and the credit card bills in the other. He crumpled them and threw them on the floor."

She stopped to catch her breath, tossed her ponytail away from her face, and continued. "My two daughters were crying, and my son looked heartbroken. Bill shouted, 'Sylvia, what in hell are you doing? You've put us in debt for over eleven thousand dollars. We need to talk! This afternoon I made some phone calls...and we know where you can get help, but you've got to make the call yourself. We can't go on like this, or we'll lose everything.' I was almost grateful that Bill had opened the letters. It meant I didn't have to lie any more and maybe they were right—maybe help was available. I slumped down on the couch and cried. I cried, my daughters cried, and even my son and my husband cried. I had a tough time trying to stop gambling and went back to the casinos many times. My husband eventually moved out. Seven weeks ago I got a letter telling us that we were losing our home. The time had come for me to start working my program. My husband and I are speaking again, and he has hinted that if I can stay away from the casinos, maybe we could try it again. I love my husband very much." Her eyes began to tear as she added, "Thank you for letting me share, and I'll be back."

Everyone clapped. Then Denise P. raised her hand. Denise never talked much, and it surprised me that she wanted to share tonight. I remembered the first time I met her. She had walked into her first meeting after not eating or sleeping for three days and could barely talk. That first night she said in a whisper, "I'm running away from home and the mess I've made. I'm planning to sleep in my car at the airport. My family doesn't know where I am. I left them a note telling them I was leaving and never coming back." A couple of us offered to take her home with us or buy her some food, but she refused. We thought she was planning to commit suicide and encouraged her to call her doctor on Barbara's cell phone. She agreed, and the next morning Denise entered a thirty-day treatment center. She'd been coming to meetings regularly for several weeks.

After putting her hand down, she said, "My name is Denise P., and I'm a compulsive gambler. I haven't gambled for sixty-three days. GA saved my life. I had planned to kill myself before I walked into my first meeting, because I couldn't face the mess I created." She took a deep breath. "I became a person I hated, and I couldn't even look in a mirror. I neglected my family and lied to them. I took money from our savings account to gamble. But thanks to this program, I'm learning how to live without gambling. GA has taught me that I am a good person, and I am learning how to forgive myself for what I've done. I know I've a long way to go, but I have the time now that I'm not gambling. And I'll be back."

Brenda's hand went up next. She had been attending meetings for almost two years now. She had told me that the only improvement in her life was that she didn't gamble. Her sharing was always the same; she constantly complained about her problems with her kids and about her husband not understanding her. We never heard her say how Brenda was doing, only about her family's problems. I had started to raise my hand, but when I saw Brenda's hand go up, I pulled mine down. Maybe tonight Brenda would say something about herself.

"Hello, my name is Brenda O., and I'm a compulsive gambler. My husband is still looking for a job, but he never leaves the house. He thinks someone will come knocking at the door and tell him to come to work. My eighteen-year-old daughter is pregnant again, and the sixteen-year-old quit school. I just don't know what to do. They've all got such crappy attitudes, and they won't listen to me. I come to this meeting every week, and nothing has changed. Where are all the miracles that everyone talks about? I know I don't call any of you on the phone, but you don't want to hear about my problems. And I know I should get a sponsor, but I don't know who to ask, and I'm afraid they'll say no if I ask them. Everyone tells me I should start working the steps, but my husband has to get a job. And I'll be back."

Poor Brenda, I thought. Can't she hear what she's saying? We know we can't change anyone else, only ourselves. We have to accept our families as they are. When we start to work the program and change ourselves, they'll learn from our example.

Mary M. raised her hand next. Everyone loved Mary because of her honesty. Her positive therapy made everyone feel better. She applied the principles of the program in every area of her life. "Hi, my name is Mary M., and I'm a compulsive gambler."

Everyone said, "Hello Mary."

"I haven't gambled for five years. When I came to my first meeting, everyone told me to get a sponsor, a female sponsor who had worked the steps. They told me to use the phone list, attend as many meetings as possible, and get involved. I made coffee, put up the chairs, became a secretary and then a treasurer. I talk to many of my GA friends several times during the week and meet some

of them for lunch. I find that I don't like 'normal' people anymore."
She paused for a minute and everyone laughed. "I guess I don't
trust anyone who doesn't have a program. When I walked into my
first meeting, no one judged me, and they all said they knew how
I felt. I didn't think anyone else in the world did the things I did.
They said if I heard something I hadn't done, to add the word 'yet,'
because if I kept gambling I would do all of the things they talked
about. When they asked me the twenty questions, I said no to question 10: Did you ever borrow to finance your gambling? But after a
few meetings, I understood that when I used my credit card in the
casino, I was borrowing money from the credit card company. And
question 16: Have you ever committed, or considered committing,
an illegal act to finance gambling? I answered no, but I found out
later that when I wrote hot checks with no money in my account,
it was an illegal act. I didn't realize that people can go to jail for
doing that. And to the two newcomers, if you want what we have,
you have to do what we do. If we work as hard on our recovery as
we did on our gambling, we'll do just fine. I'm glad I'm here, and I
never want to have to stop gambling again, and I'll be back."

Rosie raised her hand, and Barbara said, "Yes, Rosie." We all
knew that Rosie was working really hard to turn her life around.
Brenda was reaching for the Kleenex box, because she knew Rosie
wouldn't get through her therapy without breaking into tears.

"My name is Rosie B., and I'm a compulsive gambler. I know
I've been coming here for a long time, and I'm not doing very well.
My husband moved out, and my kids won't even talk to me. I went
to the casino again last night and lost my whole paycheck. I thought
if I were careful, I could make enough to send the car payment
and pay the rent. I gambled for two hours, and I was far enough
ahead so I could have paid both bills. But I couldn't stop." As the
tears streamed down Rosie's cheeks, Brenda pushed the Kleenex
box across the table. She wiped her tears and said, "I had enough
money…I should have left…I thought I was on a lucky streak, and
I should stay until it turned bad. I kept winning, and I was so happy
even though I knew I shouldn't be there. An hour later I started to
lose. It went so fast! I didn't realize it was all gone, until I started
scraping the bottom of my purse. I lost all the money. I don't know

what I'm going to do. I guess I'll talk to my landlord tomorrow and see what he says. He'll probably wait for the rent—he's done that before. But the car dealer told me if I was late again he'd take the car back. My brother won't lend me any more money, because I never pay him back. I can't pawn my rings—they're in the pawn shop already. I wish I were dead." Rosie started shaking and crying so hard she couldn't talk anymore.

Barbara told her we would talk to her after the meeting. Then she said, "The floor is open. Who's next?" The new gal, Janet, raised her hand.

"My name is Janet, and I guess I'm a compulsive gambler. I've never done anything like this before. I don't know what's happening to me. I've always been a good wife and mother to my four kids. In the last two years everything has turned really bad. One of my sons is away at college, and the other one is in the Navy, and one of our daughters just got married. Our youngest daughter is still living with us. My husband is a good man, and he works really hard, but he travels a lot. About two years ago a couple of my friends asked me if I wanted to go with them to a casino, and I said okay. No one was home that night, and I didn't have anything to do. Besides I was a little lonesome. We had a wonderful time, and I only played the nickel machine.

"Two weeks later they called me again, and I jumped at the chance. This happened about a dozen times, and I was having fun and always came home with a little extra money. Then one day I was alone and decided that maybe I could drive there by myself. Just to relax a little. I left at nine in the morning, and I didn't get home until midnight. I didn't even stop to eat. I felt really bad, because I had lost a lot of money. It wasn't that we couldn't afford it, but I felt really bad about it. I kept doing this for over a year, and sometimes I would win, but most of the time I lost.

"No one in my family knew about my gambling, because they were never home. I didn't think I was hurting anyone, and it was relaxing. Well, it wasn't really relaxing, because I had these terrible guilt feelings." She grabbed a handful of Kleenex and quickly covered her face. The room was quiet until she could talk again. I thought, *how respectful the women are by not talking when a member shares her story. No one is trying to help the newcomer finish her sentences. Everyone is allowing her to take her time and no one is interrupting her train of thought.*

Again Janet started. "I did something really terrible a couple of months ago. I drove to the bank and opened our safe deposit box and took my mother-in-law's jewelry and pawned it. I told the man in the pawn shop that I needed it to pay off a car, so we could buy another one. I lied for the first time, and I've been telling lots of lies since that afternoon. I've managed to pay the interest on the loan, but I don't know what I'm going to do next. I saw the GA phone number at the casino and thought I might find some help here."

She started crying hard again. "Janet," Barbara said, "we're glad you're here, and we hope you keep coming back. If you give us ninety days of coming to meetings without gambling, we can show you how you can turn your life around. Then if you decide you don't like what we have or you don't feel better, you can go back to gambling. The casinos will still be there. We'll give you a meeting list and a phone list, and after the meeting we all go for coffee and we'd love to have you join us so we can get to know you better." Janet nodded in agreement.

Jenny raised her hand. I hoped maybe she would lighten things up a little. It had been a really emotional meeting so far. I knew Jenny would say something that would make us laugh. She's got such a good program, and with twenty-six months in recovery, she's got a really neat sense of humor.

"Hi! My name is Jenny, and I'm a grateful recovering compulsive gambler. Welcome to the two newcomers. I remember my first night in the program. I listened to everyone sharing their stories, and I thought, I'm not like all you people, and what am I doing here? But I listened—thank God—and I heard someone say that I wouldn't ever have to gamble again if I didn't want to. So I didn't gamble again, because I thought I wasn't supposed to. I remembered saying when I lost money at the casino, I was helping put the little Indian kids through college, and my money was going for a good cause. The last time I came home from the casino, my husband was waiting up for me. I walked into the kitchen and said,

'Bill, don't say a word! There's nothing you can say that I haven't said to myself a hundred times on the way home, and now I'm going to bed!' He didn't say a word, but we've had some pretty heated discussions since then.

"Before I came to GA, I remember the nights when Bill worked out of town. I used to try so hard not to go to the casinos. Sometimes at three o'clock in the morning I'd get up, get dressed, grab my lucky rabbit's foot and my dried wishbone, and race out to the casino. At eight o'clock in the morning I'd call my job and tell them I was sick and wouldn't be in that day. I finally lost my job because I was late so many times and took so much time off. I just told myself I didn't like the job anyway. When I did go to work, all I thought about was the money I lost and the money I was going to win. And if I won, Bill would be proud of me that I was such a good gambler. Thank God I don't have to gamble today, and I'll be back."

Barbara turned to Shirley and asked, "Shirley, would you like to introduce yourself and tell us what brought you here tonight?"

"My name is Shirley T., and I don't think I'm a compulsive gambler. I think it's great that everyone here is so honest, but I haven't done any of the things you women have. I haven't lost all our money or a job or my family. I just have bad luck when I go to the casino. So after listening to you people, I'll just stay away from the casinos and none of this will happen to me." And Shirley didn't say any more.

"Shirley," Barbara said, "we're glad you came tonight, and we hope you'll attend a few more meetings. But if you've decided you're not a compulsive gambler, we'll respect your decision. Just remember, if any of the things you heard here ever happen to you, you're welcome to come back and join us." Barbara pushed her chair back and said, "And now will you all stand and join me in the 'Serenity Prayer'?

"God grant me the serenity to accept the things I cannot change, the courage to change the things I can, and the wisdom to know the difference."

Barbara gave us all a big smile and said, "You're all welcome to join us at IHOP for a cup of coffee. Sometimes the best therapy is over coffee after the meeting. We'll see you all next week." The women helped stack the chairs, and then we headed for IHOP. On the way to the restaurant, I thought to myself, *gee, I didn't share tonight.* When I first attended the meetings I was too embarrassed to talk, and then after a couple of years, I felt like the forgotten child if I wasn't called on. Now I'm content to listen to others.

One night we asked the women for some suggestions on how the men could help create a welcome atmosphere for the female gamblers. Here are the questions we suggested the male gamblers could ask themselves:

1. Do I speak to her as though she is just another gambler like me?

2. Do I speak to her at all?

3. Do I let her know that this is a fellowship, a friendship, a place of trust, and not a social club where boy meets girl?

4. Do I let her know that she can speak in any words she wishes, and that some of us swear, because it helps to vent our anger at the disease, not at anyone personally?

5. When one of my brothers shows resentment toward women in general and one in particular, do I tell her that "all men in the room do not feel this way, and we want you here, and we care that you make it in the program"?

6. Do I call her and have several others do so, at least for the first two weeks in the program?

7. Do I invite her out for coffee with the group after the meeting?

8. Do I assure her that anything she did in her past life can be talked about here, and she will not be judged, and it will not be repeated?

9. Do I tell her that whatever she did to get money to feed her habit, someone else did it before and will do it again unless she's there when the next woman comes in and can hear her story?

10. Do I speak up when a brother thinks she's not really a problem gambler and tries to discourage her from being there?

11. Do I tell her that if someone makes a pass at her, she should tell him that if he does it again, she will tell a trusted servant, because that's not the reason she's here?

12. No matter what, she must keep coming back for at least ninety days, and after that, if she hasn't found the support she needs, she can try another way?

13. Do I tell her she is loved here like a true sister, that she can hug a brother, hold his hand, and sit next to him knowing that he is her true brother and nothing but concern is being shown?

Most women (not all) are escape gamblers and not action gamblers. Women don't usually gamble for excitement. Escape gamblers usually play slot machines, bingo, or video poker and gamble for relief from a problem or pressures in their lives. Action gamblers usually gamble on card games, race tracks, or sports betting. Occasionally the action gamblers find difficulty in identifying with the escape gamblers, but after listening to everyone's therapy, both types of gamblers understand that the problems and the pain are identical.

If a new GA group doesn't leap from three members to fifteen in the first couple of weeks, don't be discouraged. The first women's group in Arizona took two years to take off. At those first meetings, we had a small core of women who came each week, but once word was out that we had found some solid recovery, other women began attending regularly.

While some women relate to the entire *Gamblers Anonymous Combo Book*, others feel they live in a different "dream world" than the one described in the book. Instead of "servants, penthouses... yachts and world tours," the dream world for a woman may involve rescuing family members and friends, paying bills, and having her own spending money.

As women listen to male gamblers' stories of beginning to gamble at early ages, gambling for thirty or forty years, and winning and losing hundreds of thousands of dollars, many notice that they have very different stories from those of a lot of male gamblers. However, as time passes and women experience more time in recovery, they realize that regardless of surface differences, all compulsive gamblers—female and male—share the same pain from their addiction. At the same time, many women recognize that they have issues and concerns they can share comfortably only with other women.

Not all female gamblers will identify with or wish to participate in women's groups; however, for some, joining a women's group may be the best way to begin recovery. In the late 1980s, California and Nevada started monthly women's groups. The Phoenix weekly women's group started on June 19, 1992. Today, several weekly women's groups meet around the United States, and spiritual energy fills the meeting rooms. The women discover as they share their stories that they are not alone. They learn that other women also gambled in an effort to escape feelings of loneliness, pain, and confusion, to find relief from stressful situations, and to replace boredom with excitement.

Many women who come to their first women's meeting feeling defeated and discouraged—in some cases, even suicidal—find support, encouragement, and hope. Some women who have always been dependent on others gain independence and a sense of empowerment for the first time in their lives. The women experience a newfound confidence and establish a powerful bond with other members in women's groups.

One of our newer members, Debbie, had been coming to meetings for four weeks when she asked if I would meet her at JB's Restaurant for a cup of coffee. She was waiting in a booth at the far corner of the restaurant, and two cups of coffee sat on the table. I had no sooner sat down when she leaned across the booth and whispered, "Marilyn, how did you stop gambling?"

"Well, I guess I had to first decide whether or not I had a problem."

"How did you come to that decision?"

"The first step in the *Combo Book* reads, 'We admitted we were powerless over gambling—and our lives had become unmanageable.' My sponsor and I sat at his kitchen table and talked about how he made his decision. Just like we're doing now. He suggested I take a sheet of paper, make two columns on it, and label one, 'Admitted I was powerless over gambling,' and the other one, 'My life had become unmanageable.' And then he told me to open the *Combo Book* to the twenty questions and go through them one at a time and write out my answers on the paper."

"It sounds complicated," she said with a sigh.

"Only until you have the paper and pencil in front of you. I remember when I wrote my first step, it was almost like someone moved the pencil for me. And then all of a sudden, I became painfully honest and couldn't stop writing. It was like emptying out a huge trash barrel. The first question—'Did you ever lose time from work due to gambling?'—I quickly answered no, because I never missed time from work. I had to be there every day to cover up the mess I created in the office bookkeeping records. What I later realized was that I always had my mind on the weekend trip to Laughlin. So I wasn't at work mentally. And when I finished the twenty questions, I admitted I was powerless over gambling and my life was unmanageable."

"I guess I can do that. I know I tried stopping on my own dozens of times, and it never worked. I've been pretending the problem would just go away."

After three cups of coffee, with a heavy sigh Debbie picked up her purse and her *Combo Book*, and we gave each other a big hug and walked to our cars. As she opened her car door, she turned to me, and with a hesitant smile, she said, "I'll see you at the meeting tomorrow night."

On my way home I recalled the day I left my sponsor's home and headed to my apartment to work on my first step. I guess this is why the members say, "You've got to give it away to keep it." I felt stronger after my chat with Debbie in the restaurant. I knew it would be a lot of work for Debbie, but so was gambling.

I smiled as I recalled my first few weeks in the program and the slow progress I made. But I thank God that recovery is as progressive as the gambling addiction was.

9

Biggest Win of All
(A Recap)

Recovery is a gift, and my recovery from compulsive gambling proved to be the biggest win in my lifetime. I still enjoy meetings, and I'm so grateful to Dr. Bob and Bill W. for starting the first twelve-step program. Where else could I go and listen to ninety minutes of sharing and therapy for only one dollar and learn how to turn my life around? While I gambled, I thought gambling relaxed me. When angry, I thought it calmed me down, and when I was happy, I celebrated by gambling. Gambling became my *coping mechanism*. By attending meetings, I learned how to replace that *coping mechanism* with *coping skills*.

The GA program is made up of Twelve Recovery Steps, which are the principles of the program and guide each individual through a healing process. The Twelve Unity Steps help organize the individual GA groups and contain guidelines to ensure that the structure of each GA group is consistent. Some members may have difficulty at their first few meetings and may go back to gambling for a short time, while some find the answers to their questions at their first meetings. Fortunately for me, I never returned to the casinos after my first meeting. I sometimes have thoughts of gambling, but it has never gone beyond the thoughts. Perhaps it was because of the years I had been a member of AA or maybe because when I hit my bottom, my life was so painful and devastating. The struggle inside me was greater than the struggle with outside is-sues, so I needed to stop gambling. I constantly hear the words at meetings, "I'm not responsible for my first thought, but I am responsible for what I do with it."

Life hasn't always run smoothly since I stopped gambling, but it wasn't trouble-free when I gambled. *After* I stopped gambling, I lost my home, my retirement, and my freedom. My mother died two weeks after my arrest. At that time I learned that there was no problem that would present itself that gambling wouldn't make worse. My son died six months after my release from prison, and my boyfriend died one year later. I didn't have to gamble over those painful experiences.

There will always be traumatic incidents in life and having someone tell me to "stop worrying" doesn't help. When a crisis oc-curs today, I rely on my Higher Power and the program. I still write in my journal and find it to be a cleansing process. I carry a small notepad and pencil in my car and in my purse and keep one on my bedside table. Writing in my journal helps me decide if I'm put-ting too much emphasis on any issues. There are days when I'm not aware of stress or tension until I feel the tightening of my muscles or the beginning of a headache. Here are some methods I've used to help reduce my stress and work through painful issues.

For instant relief, I find relaxation through deep-breathing ex-ercises, reciting the "Serenity Prayer," taking a walk, making a tele-phone call to someone in the program, or finding a quiet place to sit for a moment. Laughing helps if I can find something to laugh about.

When I have the *time*, I can set the stage with soft lighting and a scented candle and experience aromatherapy. I can enjoy a mas-sage, take a leisurely bath, meditate, or listen to motivational tapes. For *long-term* relief I can eat balanced meals, sleep regular hours, and try to change the patterns in my life that cause stress.

Attending meetings when I'm stressed always helps. When I sit in a meeting, I usually hear a new word or phrase or a new definition for an old word or saying. I made a list of some words and phrases that are used frequently in the program, and I'd like to share my abbreviated definitions and explain how they relate to my life. If anyone wishes to read more on one of the topics, the shelves in the bookstores are filled with dozens of books on each word listed here.

Abstinence: The existence between my addiction and my recovery; the period where there are no pleasures or rewards. Some members call it "white knuckling." When I began attending meetings I really didn't want to change anything, only to control my gambling. My vocabulary was filled with "shouldn't," "couldn't," "won't work," "can't," and "you don't understand." After I stopped gambling, I was still miserable and I made those around me miserable. Denying my anger, resentment, guilt, and remorse didn't make them disappear, so I followed the suggestion of my sponsor and began to look at my character defects.

Acceptance: The basic recovery concept that never loses its power to work miracles is called *acceptance*. Acceptance is my decision to willingly approve certain situations in my life. I didn't achieve acceptance in a quick minute. I often worked through my list of feelings—anger, outrage, shame, self-pity, or sadness. Repeating the "Serenity Prayer" several times helped in deciding if there was a solution to the problem or if the issue was beyond my control.

Addict: A person who is dependent on a substance or action and devotes oneself excessively or compulsively.

Addiction: A chronic disorder characterized by the repeated use of a substance or behavior, despite evidence of harm to oneself or of unhealthy consequences. An addiction isn't logical, so it doesn't respond to reason. The gambling addiction is progressive and easy to hide. It not only causes pain to the gambler but to everyone around him or her. If something looked good, felt good, or tasted good, I became addicted. I was your regular housewife and next-door neighbor, but I lied and cheated to get money to continue gambling. You probably didn't know what I was doing; my family didn't even know.

Changing fear to faith: Most of us came to Gamblers Anonymous carrying our own private collection of fears. We feared losing family, home, freedom, and sanity. We had no idea how to deal with the fear! I remember saying at my first meeting, "But you don't understand what I'm going through!"

Other members told us, "One day at a time," and, "Don't try to solve all your problems at once." It's not easy for a compulsive gambler to summon up a bit of faith. We can't fake it. It begins with finding a power greater than ourselves.

Many GA members identify their Higher Power as the traditional God. Others believe in a supreme being but choose to call their deity by another name. Still others designate their GA room or the fellowship as their Higher Power. If the power we identify resides within, then we have nowhere to place our faith but in ourselves…and we've seen where that got us!

Some of us wonder, "How am I supposed to have faith? I don't even know what faith *is*." Faith is difficult to define, but if we have fear, we don't have faith, and if we have faith, we don't have fear.

Choices: Trapped in the downward spiral of compulsive gambling, many women feel as if they have no choice. A respected GA member with well over twenty years of abstinence *and* recovery once said in a meeting, "I used to have no choice. I had to gamble. But once I went to my first Gamblers Anonymous meeting, I had a *choice*." Yes, we have a choice about whether or not to gamble. Of course, when we choose not to, we're choosing to take on a job as difficult as any we have ever tackled, but we don't have to do the job alone.

We have choices about virtually every aspect of our lives. A woman in an abusive relationship chooses either to leave or to remain. A woman with a paycheck pays the mortgage and buys groceries, when she could have chosen to go to the casino. A woman in the throes of a gambling addiction can choose to surrender to the addiction or to seek help. We can choose to allow the addiction to destroy us or choose recovery, which is available through the twelve recovery steps.

Communication: When I was in the throes of my gambling, I delivered mixed messages that confused everyone. I might tell you that I didn't want to go gambling this weekend, so you could convince me why we should go. I was being manipulative and lacked sensitivity. I alienated my family and friends. I listened to you but I didn't hear what you were saying. Because I was a poor listener I usually misinterpreted the meaning of your message, or I just didn't want to hear what you were saying, because it may have been disturbing. I finished sentences for you, assuming I knew more than you did.

Some of the GA members shared their methods for effective listening, which include: maintain eye contact; observe the speaker's verbal and nonverbal communication; keep an open mind; eliminate prejudice from your thoughts; and don't jump to conclusions. In addition, try to withhold judgment until the message is completed, resist distractions, and think before you speak.

Denial: This is to the mind what physical shock is to the body. Denial is an automatic psychological process by which we protect ourselves from something that threatens us, the same as physical shock protects us from feeling immediate pain when we're injured. We can replace denial by truth and acceptance and not minimize or rationalize. Denial is as progressive as the gambling addiction and impairs our judgment. We aren't even sure what's true or false and sometimes delude ourselves. We blame others and may become hostile, but with hard work and following the GA program, we can develop a healthier lifestyle. There's always the question, are we in denial or simply unaware. If we're made to be aware of the problem, and we still don't comply or believe, then it's probably denial.

Filling the void: Gambling compulsively consumed my life for seven long years. I used gambling to avoid problems or to inject excitement into my life. I spent *time* on it. The early days in the program found me with *time* on my hands. We may not remember what activities filled our hours before gambling. How do we get our life back?

When I joined GA, I attended meetings five or six nights a

week. I needed the therapy to heal the pain. When I felt secure in my recovery, I enrolled in a local college, something I had wanted to do since high school. I saved money to buy a home, I bought a digital camera and took photography classes, and I took some belly dancing classes. When I moved into my new home, I joined a garden club and transformed my backyard into an oasis. I found a part-time job close to my home, and I enjoy the work and meeting people. Some days I wonder where I ever found the time to gamble.

Grief: Several members told me that when I stopped gambling I would go through a grieving period. They were right. How do we grieve? Awkwardly, imperfectly, usually with a great deal of resistance, and often with anger and attempts to negotiate. Ultimately, we surrender to the pain. The grief process is a five-stage process: denial, anger, bargaining, sadness, and finally, acceptance. I became a hospice volunteer a couple of years ago, and during the training period, I was fortunate to receive an in-depth study on how to handle grief and grieving. The class gave me a whole new perspective on accepting death.

When we talk about "unfinished business," it refers to when we have not completed grieving. We're stuck somewhere in the grief process. Usually, the place where we become stuck is denial. Passing through denial is the first and most dangerous stage of grieving, but it is also the first step toward acceptance.

I received many sympathy cards through the years, and I copied some of the verses that had a positive impact on me:

You sit in the shadow of sorrow, searching for the magic that will make the pain go away. Everything you feel is appropriate, there is no right way to grieve—there is just your way.

It will take as long as it takes.

Be gentle with yourself, and let others be gentle to you.

No one ever said it was easy to let go, let be, let life do what it is supposed to do.

You will be healed, the pain will go away, and the sun will shine again, and you will stop asking why.

Jealousy and Envy: Most emotions have their good and bad characteristics, but not jealousy. It is all bad. Jealous members are motivated by fear, mistrust, and resentment. We have no peace of mind. We lack faith in GA. We do not trust God or our fellow members. Jealousy and criticism have broken up a lot of twelve-step groups.

Jealousy of another individual can prey upon the human mind until, like a cancer, it injures or destroys. When I concentrate on what I don't have, I feel inferior. I start to run myself down and feel jealous of other people. There will always be people who have better *things* than I do, but nobody can take away the good that's inside of me.

I can't be jealous and grateful at the same time. I'm a good person, and the more I respect myself, the easier it will be to accept good things in the lives of other people. Jealousy is a lot like self-pity and can make us feel selfish and self-centered.

When we compare ourselves to others, the destruction is far greater than our conscious minds are aware of. Envy interferes with all of our interactions. It possesses all of our thoughts and denies us the freedom to achieve that which can be ours.

Positive Thinking: To begin work on our recovery, we must be open-minded. We need to develop an attitude of honesty and rid ourselves of denial, deceit, taking shortcuts, holding on to old ideas, and being satisfied with half-measures. When I began to understand and work on my recovery, my attitudes and outlook began to change.

The price I paid for sitting in the chair at each meeting was high, monetarily, emotionally, and spiritually. Monetarily, the cost was in the thousands. Emotionally and spiritually, the damage couldn't be calculated. But I wouldn't trade a day of recovery for one day of gambling. I know if I go back out and gamble, there are no guarantees that I'll have the desire to come back to the program. I know I will have to start the hard work all over again. So, "one day at a time," I will not gamble.

Principles Before Personalities: The twelfth step in the Unity Program contains the words "principles before personalities," and assures us of direction in our lives. The GA history mentions, "They used for a guide certain spiritual principles which had been utilized by thousands of people who were recovering from other compulsive addictions." Page 3 of the *Combo Book* tells us, "In order to lead normal happy lives, we try to practice to the best of our ability, certain principles in our daily affairs." Page 13 in the *Combo Book* reads, "Adherence to spiritual principles seems to solve our problems." We are a part of a fellowship, and a focus on *personalities* could undermine the good of the whole. Anonymity plays an important part in the twelfth unity step. Page 4 of *GA—A New Beginning* says, "Anonymity has tremendous spiritual significance. It represents a powerful reminder that we need always place principles before personalities." By practicing the principles and respecting anonymity, we assure humility, harmony, and spiritual comfort among our members.

We listen to the message and not the messenger. We read on page two of the *GA Combo Book* that, "The only requirement for membership is a desire to stop gambling." We respect the opinions of others and avoid gossip and prejudice. An old twelve-step saying expresses our aim well: "Say what you mean, mean what you say, but don't be mean when you say it."

Our GA principles protect our fellowship and ensure us a solid foundation. *A New Beginning* (page 57) says, "We understand that what is best for the group is best for each individual." Our GA program will not be destroyed from outside forces but could be destroyed from within if we do not respect the twelfth unity step and practice principles before personalities.

Recovery: Abstinence alone is not enough, but it must come first. For a short time I hung on to the old way of life, because it was familiar. The fear of the unknown controlled me. Recovery was a healing process, and with it came spiritual growth, a new freedom, and happiness. During my recovery, I learned the meanings of honesty, open-mindedness, and willingness.

The Random House College Dictionary defines recovery as "the regaining of something lost or taken away." Some of the things taken away from us by our addictions are choices, serenity, self-confidence, and spirituality.

As we begin to chase away the shame and guilt, we start making choices. We learn to trust and love ourselves and others. When we gambled, we created walls that kept us apart from our friends and family.

We cannot settle for being an "almost person," almost living up to our potentials or capabilities. We try harder and put as much effort into our recovery as we did into our addiction, because if we only work the program part of the time the program will only work for us part of the time. And that part of the time when we desperately need it, it may not be there.

When I was new in the program, I often sat and listened for others, thinking, "Boy, I hope Mary is listening," or "Jane could use this." After some time, I began listening for myself.

Rhythm: Working the twelve steps is the process of being and becoming. It is finding, knowing, and accepting who we are. It is having the willingness to fall down, stumble around, and make mistakes. Each of us has an internal timetable—the rhythm of our spirit. Discovering what it is and living according to its direction can bring us untold serenity and joy. It also brings us energy, because we're not fighting ourselves.

Self-esteem: "We'll love you until you learn to love yourself." These words, heard so often in our meetings, promise a day we look forward to—the day when we'll know how to love ourselves. We all want this elusive quality as soon as we hear about it. Some of us seem to stumble upon it accidentally, while others embark on a course of action complete with affirmations. Fix-it-yourself techniques and trendy psychological cures can only take us so far. There are some definite steps we can take to show love for ourselves and begin paying attention to our own needs.

Spirituality: A spiritual awakening offered me the ability to see what I was looking at, to hear what I was listening to, and to feel what I touched. Life was no longer a blur.

Various definitions for spirituality abound. Ask any ten people to define it, and you'll probably hear ten definitions. A common thread through most definitions is connectedness—a feeling of being connected with our families and friends, with GA members, and most important, with our Higher Power. Despite years of gambling compulsively, we all have a tiny kernel of spirituality remaining within, because we were born with it.

The *GA Combo Book* emphasizes that ours is a *spiritual* program, not a religious one. Most of us believe that religion produces spirituality—that a person who is religious is automatically spiritual. Nothing could be further from the truth. A person can have religion without spirituality, and one can also grow in spirituality without choosing to be involved with organized religion.

A full submission to the reality of step 1—powerlessness and unmanageability—can provide abstinence from gambling, but *recovery* requires spirituality. The first page of the *Combo Book* says, "The word spiritual can be said to describe those characteristics of the human mind that represent the highest and finest qualities such as kindness, generosity, honesty, and humility."

Four months before his death, Dr. Bob, cofounder of Alcoholics Anonymous, said:

> There are two or three things that flashed into my mind on which it would be fitting to lay a little emphasis; one is the simplicity of our program. Let's not louse it all up with Freudian complexes and things that are interesting to the scientific mind, but have very little to do with our actual AA work....

Sponsors: A sponsor was a person in the group who helped me work the steps and answered my questions. Having a sponsor was important. A sponsor needs to be someone you trust and respect. For me, it had to be a person I identified with and felt comfortable talking to. My sponsor took me to new meetings and introduced me to other members, reviewed the twelve steps with me, and encouraged me to keep an open mind.

Working the Program: Before GA I was always about to do something or thinking about doing something, but I rarely did anything. Working the program consists of understanding the *Combo Book* and other GA literature, applying the twelve recovery and unity steps to our lives, attending meetings, and, when we are ready, performing service work. We can learn how to live in the "now" rather than in the future or the past.

If we use the telephone and meeting lists we're given, we discover we're no longer alone. GA members encourage us to use the telephone *before* trouble visits us. If we follow the advice in the *Combo Book:* our lives will get better. Page 17 has a list of seven suggestions we should follow if we want recovery. They are:

1. Attend as many meetings as possible, but at least one full meeting per week. Meetings make it.

2. Telephone other members as often as possible between meetings. Use the telephone list!

3. Don't test or tempt yourself. Don't associate with acquaintances who gamble. Don't go in or near gambling establishments. Don't gamble for anything. This includes the stock market, commodities, options, buying or playing lottery tickets, raffle tickets, flipping a coin, or entering the office sport pool.

4. Live the Gamblers Anonymous Program One Day at a Time. Don't try to solve all your problems at once.

5. Read the Recovery and Unity Steps often and continuously review the Twenty Questions. Follow the steps in your daily affairs. These steps are the basis for the entire Gamblers Anonymous Program and practicing them is the key to your growth. If you have any questions, ask them of your Trusted Servants and Sponsors.

6. When you are ready the Trusted Servants will conduct a Pressure Relief Group meeting, or re-evaluation for you and your spouse (if married), and adherence to it will aid in your recovery.

7. Be patient! The days and weeks will pass soon enough, and as you continue to attend meetings and abstain from gambling, your recovery will really accelerate.

Remember, if we go back to gambling, we don't return to the level where we began—we start where we left off. Working the program doesn't mean only selected parts. It means working the entire program. And it truly is work, but it will be some of the most rewarding work we perform during our entire lives.

10

Articles by Counselors and Gamblers

The following articles appeared in past issues of the *Women Helping Women* newsletter, and I thank the writers for giving me permission to include them in my book. The first eight letters were written by recovering compulsive gamblers or their families. I am grateful to the many women who submitted articles. Without their contributions, the newsletter would not exist. There were about three hundred letters from which to choose, making the choices difficult.

The Best Is Yet to Come (February 2000)

My name is Lynne H., a grateful compulsive gambler, in recovery and bet free for over twenty-one years. I will never forget my last gambling binge. It was Thanksgiving time, and I gambled continuously for seven days—no change of clothing and no shower. I chose to gamble rather than have dinner with my daughters. They always knew where I was.

I experienced my first gambling episode November 30, 1952, first night of my honeymoon spent at the tables. I learned to play blackjack from my husband at the time. I had credit for the first time in my life and also had markers. The only vacations we had were in Las Vegas or some other gambling resort. When my daughters were thirteen and fourteen, we took them to Las Vegas for the first time. I dressed them up fancy, playing like the proud parent; I gave them $10 each to play the slot machines. Now, we were free to gamble. This was my life for many years.

I got divorced about twenty-two years ago, and my gambling accelerated. My children were in college, and I was free to do whatever I wanted. Guess what? I gambled compulsively—until I came to GA November 23, 1978. I gambled on the twenty-third, so I count my days from the twenty-fourth. My GA birthday is in November, and my natal birthday is in November also. In my heart, I feel I was reborn. Vince, my sponsor from the first night, directed me. I followed direction for the first time in my life. Gamblers Anonymous saved my life.

When I had ninety days, I was asked to chair my first meeting. This was such an honor. I learned early from Vince that service is healing. The first year I went to a meeting daily. My life changed. I give service and I'm there for the newcomer. I followed Vince, did what he did. I was a secretary, a trustee, and on the board of regents. I love myself today. It feels good to tell my story in print. GOD BLESS GAMBLERS ANONYMOUS, THE BEST IS YET TO COME!!!!!

—Lynne H., California

Theory on Hitting Bottom (July 1999)

I am one of the ones many GA members call "lucky," blessed with maintaining abstinence from my very first GA meeting. However, I really believe that I understand why some people relapse multiple times before they put together a significant period of time not gambling. Here is my theory about hitting bottom.

You know, we all have pain and demons. That is a part of life. Some of us just fail to cope with it in a healthy way and end up seeking refuge in some form of substance-based or behavior-based altering of brain chemistry. We are self-anesthetizing.

DEFINITION: Bottom happens when the pain created by the behavior you have adopted to anesthetize your pain becomes greater than the pain you initially set out to escape. I got to my bottom, and then walked into my first meeting. Others come in earlier in the cycle. They certainly know that gambling is causing pain, no longer giving them the shelter from it. But they come in at a point before the pain from gambling is worse than their initial pain. These women go back out, and then, once enough misery from gambling piles up, the scale tips, and they have endured enough. They have found bottom and can now truly embrace recovery.

So I am always troubled when new members berate themselves for relapsing. They seem to feel that those of us who "got it" from our first meeting are somehow superior. I argue, however, that women like me are the ones who really took longer to get it. We are the ones who went all the way down before we took our first step toward help and hope.

—Carol R., Arizona

Path of Self-Destruction (July 1999)

As you have read in this newsletter, many, if not most, women are "escape gamblers." I personally have about equal parts action gambler and escape gambler in my makeup. My games of choice were poker and blackjack. I got a real rush from the moment I hit the casino, a feeling of exhilaration that it seemed I could almost literally trace would run through my bloodstream. To this day I can still recall the sensation. But I undoubtedly was compelled by a desire to leave my pain and demons at the door and find a few hours of peace at the casino, even when I swore I would never return.

Like you, I knew I was locked into a path of self-destruction. I tried to quit on my own a million times. I was completely confounded by my inability to control whether or not I would end up at the casino on any given day. At the end, I simply had no ability to stop myself from going. Until June 8, 1995.

I went on a binge to the brand new Harrah's in New Orleans. I lied, and said I was there on a business trip, but it was a binge, pure and simple. For three days and nights I drank and gambled. (I am a double winner—recovering alcoholic, too.) I had completely concealed these facts from EVERYONE. I was totally in the closet with my drinking and gambling. Imagine the lies I told my partner, covering up this daily lifestyle.

By the end of the three days, I was completely debased. I had lost thousands of dollars. I was sick from the alcohol and lack of sleep. I had reached the point where I was so sick of who I had become, so to-the-bone disgusted with my lies and deceiving the people I loved. I lay in the bed in the hotel and cried until every drop of moisture left my body, and I still kept on crying. I replayed in my brain all of the horror of the last two years of my descent into hell. In that moment, I knew how utterly alone I was and that I could not go on. I had hit bottom.

—Carol R., Arizona (*Read Carol's partner's story below.*)

...Until I Found the Journal (August 1999)

After four years, my alcoholic partner solemnly announced that she was sober. I was completely delighted. What a tribute to my steadfast devotion. My love had conquered her addiction. I had never felt more successful and spent the next two years believing I was the happiest woman on earth...until I found the journal. I didn't understand it. I read on...casino...$30,000...lost...devastated...Harrah's...gambling? I read it over and over, placed it face down on the kitchen counter, and waited for her to come home. "Sweetie, I wanted to ask you something," I said.

It was not an ambush. I believed with all my heart that she was about to offer a perfectly logical, rational, explanation. I couldn't imagine what she would say, but I had complete confidence that everything would be back to normal by the time the rice was ready. I presented the journal and said in my most casual, non-accusatory tone, "What is this?"

She looked up at me through a long, tormented sob and began a litany of every major lie she had told me. Every last second of the past two years—indeed, the best two years of my life—had been a sham.

I couldn't tell you exactly what she said, but each word fell like an assault, each sentence a rape, every lie a betrayal. Lie by lie, I listened to my life's revision. Dumbfounded, I tried to speak but could only stand in silence. The silence shattered as she turned to me with the final bit of information. "And you'll be further upset to know that I've been drinking all the while."

Off I went, over the edge. The gambling, the debt, even the lies somehow hadn't yet registered. But her sobriety was my symbol of success! When that turned out to be the final lie, everything came into crystal clarity, and it hurt like hell. Her tears, apologies, and promises meant nothing. I was looking into the eyes of a total stranger. I saw nothing left of her to love, and I had nothing to lose.

For the first time, I couldn't have cared less what she thought, how she felt, or what she would do. Further, I realized deep down in my soul that I had not the slightest bit of power over what she thought, how she felt, or what she would do. I found I was able to ask: What do I think? How do I feel? What will I do? I didn't realize it at that moment, but I had just taken step one of my own recovery program.

—Denise D., Arizona (Carol's partner)

Humility—What a Concept! (April 2000)

I wish I still had my high school Latin book; I suspect it would tell me humiliation and humility share the same root word. Strange thought. We've probably all experienced the devastation of being humiliated. I know I have; in fact, some of the worst humiliations have come at my own hands. Suffering humiliation. Bad, very bad. Gaining humility. Good, very good.

Humility is one of those character assets we're taught we will develop if we consistently work a good program. What is humility? Forced to come up with a one-word synonym for humility, I would go with modesty. But the word certainly doesn't constitute a definition of humility. We're all familiar with the concept of false modesty. But when we have the pleasure of spending time with a GA sister—or brother—who has truly gained humility, unmistakable sincerity always accompanies every statement, every action.

Humility is "slippery" though! Something an "old-time" GA gentleman wrote several years ago pretty much sums up the humility quandary. He said something to this effect: "The moment I think I've got humility, it's gone!" If I start patting myself on the back for being so humble, any humility I may have genuinely allowed to develop gets shoved out the window by the pride I've taken in my humility!

Years ago, a songwriter expressed it pretty well. "Oh, Lord, it's hard to be humble when you're perfect in every way...." The words imply hard, but not impossible—being perfect in every way would, after all, require humility! It's an entertaining dichotomy in a song, but what about real life? What's an industrious, little twelve-stepper to do?

I don't have the answer. I understand just enough about humility to know it's an illusive quality. We sure can't acquire it by direct effort! That would require too much thought about a quality that flees when we become aware it's present. I think the answer—for me anyway—lies on Page 17. "Follow the steps in your daily affairs." If I follow that advice, everything else seems to take care of itself.

—Betty C., Arizona

Three Big Words (May 2003)

GA's *Combo Book* says, "Honesty, Open-Mindedness, and Willingness are the key words in our recovery." Actually, it's not the words, but the qualities, that are key to our recovery. Why?

Well, we often hear someone say, "It's a program of honesty." And it is. We were anything but honest when we were practicing our addiction. Our objective in recovery is to turn around the negative behaviors that characterized us then; it stands to reason that honesty is a quality we need to cultivate.

No need to enumerate the details of our dishonesty here. We're so much alike! Our lengthy lists would probably be quite similar. I can only speak from my own experience, so I want to address the dishonest behavior that has proved to be my biggest challenge as my recovery progresses. LYING.

One big lesson I've learned is that life is much less complicated if I tell the truth. For one thing, I don't have to expend energy and gray matter remembering what I've said! It was hard keeping all the lies straight; if I tell the truth, I've found I rarely contradict myself. But I became such a facile liar when I was gambling. Lying has proved a hard habit to break. I'm working on it.

I don't believe it's in my best interest to draw some arbitrary line, where it's okay to lie on one side of the line, but not on the other. If I draw a line, I can move the line. If it's okay this week to lie about why I didn't get the lawn mowed, next week I may decide it's okay to lie about why I didn't do a lick of work on my current writing project. I've never heard anybody say, "It's a program of selective honesty"! Like addiction and recovery, lying is progressive.

So I'm not very open-minded when it comes to lying. On many other topics, I've become much more open-minded than I used to be. It's important in GA for members to be open-minded regarding the spiritual beliefs of others. My way isn't the only way. In the beginning, we may have to be open-minded just to buy into the concept that a twelve-step recovery program can help us put the disease of pathological gambling under arrest. Many of us have to open our minds to the belief that working steps four and five will relieve us of the heavy burdens of anger, resentment, fear, and guilt that have weighed us down most of our lives. And step seven?! I'm a firm believer in open-mindedness, while at the same time placing credence in the old saying, "Don't become so open-minded that your brains fall out!"

Willingness is of equal importance with those other two key qualities. I had to be willing to admit that I simply couldn't stop gambling without asking for some help! I tried and tried and I just couldn't do it. I had to become willing to ask Wanda to sponsor me. And I became so willing that I asked Marilyn to sponsor me, too! I tell people, "I'm a tough case; I need two sponsors." I had to become willing to follow their advice—and the occasional order. I've become willing to shlep off to that extra meeting when I know I need it, whether I want to go or not. Above all, I had to become willing to change.

—Betty C., Arizona

Piercey Family Letters (November 2003)

Keith and Catherine Piercey of Corner Brook, Newfoundland, Canada, sent the following letters. Their daughter Susan is a patient at an addictions clinic and she is writing her letters from the clinic. Susan was asked to write about her personal feeling on gambling. Her letter appears in its entirety, Excerpts from her parents' letters are interspersed.

A Good-bye Letter (from Susan) written on July 23, 2003, to the Video Lottery Terminal (VLT)

Susan (to the slot machine (VLT): You were once my friend, allowing me to escape into your world with only a small price to pay (or so I thought). Your lights, music, flashing screens made me retreat into my fantasy world away from reality, time, and friends. For a long time, you filled an emptiness inside me and didn't ask for much besides money. You let me sit for hours, never questioning, always with a promise of maybe the next spin.

Catherine (Susan's mom): Her problem started as soon as these machines were introduced into this province. She started gambling all of her student loans. Later, she held down three jobs in St. John's to sustain her habit. She did not have a driver's license, and, since she gambled all of her paychecks, she had no money for bus fare or cabs. She ended up totally wiped out physically and came back to Corner Brook. We then sent her to an addiction centre in Ontario for a month. I believe now that was like a vacation for her and was not helpful.

Susan: I stayed and played on your empty promises and lost not only money, but my soul. I lost me sometimes while being mesmerized by your offer of more. I sold my soul to play your game, you never judged, ever ready to accept my money. I always knew that you would be there when I was stressed, hurt, frustrated, or just plain lonely. I came looking for love and acceptance; that and much more was taken from me.

Catherine: Every payday Susan would gamble her entire paycheck. She stayed at home, so she did not have very many expenses. She borrowed from finance companies and had student loans to repay and these companies were continuously calling for payments. My bank account was wiped out twice.

Susan: I lost my self-respect, I lost my trust in me. I lost dignity. I no longer trusted my feelings. I just became numb, oblivious to the hurt I was causing my family and myself. If you would only let me out of your clutches and allow me to reclaim my life, without constantly fighting to stay out of your grasp. Your grip is unbelievably strong, still trying to tempt me back into this insidious illness. I want to beat you, yet I know you will patiently wait for me to fail so that I will run back to you. Isn't this what I have done for years?

Catherine: We could not leave cash or checks in the house. She stole checks and credit cards from her grandmother and just about cleaned her out financially. Checks and cash were stolen from relatives staying at our house. She sold everything that she owned that could possibly be sold and things that she did not own, including a gold coin set that my father had given me when I got married. She returned Christmas gifts purchased for other people to the store and got the money.

Susan: I have to let you go, you've hurt me more than anything or anyone in my life. You made me reach depths I thought were impossible. You, with my assistance, turned me into a liar, a thief, and a con.

Catherine: Things got progressively worse, and she took money she did not have in the account out of an ATM at a local bank. The bank laid charges and the Royal Newfoundland Constabulary (RNC) became involved. Even that did nothing to instill any fear in her of what might happen. Her court date was scheduled for sometime this fall. The pending court date still did not stop her from stealing and gambling all of her money. So many people tried to help her.

Susan: I never thought I would be thirty years old going to court for fraud and writing bad checks.

Keith (Susan's dad): We have many letters written by Susan ("Dear Me") that steadily address her gambling problem.

Catherine: I've never experienced a feeling quite like the one that came over me when I was told that the RNC were on their way to my office, looking for me. My husband had tried to reach me by phone but my line was busy.

After spending time with friends the evening of July 23, and certainly not indicating anything to them, Susan tried to kill herself that night. She must have realized there was no way out and no hope of ever beating those VLTs. We would later find out that between Monday and Wednesday of that week she had stolen and gambled about $1,000.

Keith had gone to our daughter's bedroom and found her unconscious after trying to kill herself with a large dose of medication. She never regained consciousness.

Susan was thirty-one years of age. She was a beautiful, intelligent girl who always had a smile and a few words for everyone, no matter who. She adored her niece and nephew. Susan was always concerned about other people's problems. But she had a big problem of her own—gambling and VLTs.

Keith: Last week we found an article on the Internet regarding gambling on VLTs in Quebec. It said data now shows that at least one gambler in the Province commits suicide every two weeks.

Catherine: We pray for others who may have suffered and still may be suffering the same as our family has done.

Susan Jane Piercey
March 17, 1972–July 28, 2003
May she rest in peace.

Befriend Yourself (June 2003)

As I look at the picture of the two-year-old girl, I can't help but smile. Her blue eyes and dimpled smile hold a mischievous look. The chubby little hands are gently closed and perfectly balanced on her lap. Lace accents her lavender dress and socks. A lavender barrette adorns her light brown hair, and a tiny heart locket, a treasure for this very special little girl, dangles at her throat.

And the adorable shoes…black patent leather, shiny on the top, but with well-worn soles; she probably didn't often sit still in this innocent, perfectly posed position. I am drawn back to her smile and her eyes. This innocent child is genuinely happy and peaceful, perhaps holding the inner knowledge that this is a very special photograph. This dear child is "Little Betty," and because of her, I have learned the importance of loving myself and have been able to travel my journey of recovery from my gambling addiction.

Six years ago I was in a state of hopelessness. I saw no way to ease the pain from my abusive marriage except to escape to gambling when the pain became too great. My behaviors were self-destructive and hurtful to my three young sons, and yet I continued to gamble.

My psychologist and I discussed ways to stop my self-destruction. I was so concerned about stopping pain that I didn't care about the danger I was courting. As the mother of three young children and a teacher, my psychologist knew me to be very protective of my children, at home and at school. She asked if I had any pictures of me when I was a child.

I immediately thought of a picture in my baby book that I had always loved. That is when "Little Betty" moved from a box in my closet to a frame on my dresser. My counselor had suggested that every time I did something I knew would be hurtful I look at that precious child and say, "Would I want Little Betty to go through that?"

For the first couple of months I wouldn't look at Little Betty and would still make choices that hurt me, but I kept studying that trusting child.

Soon, I connected with Little Betty. When I was in great pain and wanted to run off to the casino or when I was still afraid to leave my abusive marriage, I would look at the picture of me as a happy, innocent child and say, "Do I want to put you through this, Little Betty?" From then on the answer was always a no! I couldn't hurt this child. Little Betty and I have become great friends. Countless times when I have had urges to gamble or a decision to make, I have said to her, "Little Betty, I won't hurt you." I can't hurt that little child—me. Connecting with myself through the photograph stopped my self-destruction.

It has been over five and a half years since I last gambled and over five years since I left my abusive marriage. Little Betty and I deserve the best in life!

—Love, Betty M., Arizona

Spirituality and Recovery (June 1999)

At a recent conference in Detroit, I had the wonderful experience of hearing Reverend Leo Booth, an Episcopal priest, speak on the difference between spirituality and religion in the process of healing. He dared to suggest something twelve-step programs profess: you can live without religion, but you only exist without the awareness of spirituality.

Spirituality is the way out of our isolation. It is the way out of our prison. It is the key that opens the door to ourselves. It is *that which enables and develops positive and creative forces in a human being.* People ask, "How do I get it? How do I bring spirituality into my life? Is there a teach-yourself book?" These questions miss the essential point about spirituality: spirituality has already been given. You and I have it. We are spiritual creatures, and the emphasis should not be on getting it or obtaining it but on discovering it within ourselves.

Unlocking our spirituality for many begins when we dare to be honest with ourselves. It is good for family and friends to accept that we are recovering compulsive gamblers. But it is essential for us to know and accept it and even to use the disease in our life to guide our healing. Learning to be responsible for that part of us that is diseased, that is spirituality. For to confront what is sick and unhealthy, gives us the opportunity to discover what needs to be done for our recovery.

In the acceptance of our disease are the seeds of wellness! Spirituality is knowing that we have the power to change, recognizing the force for good and wholeness in the universe, and coming to believe that through the miracle of creative effort, negatives can be turned into positives. Denial becomes acceptance; depression turns to hope; manipulation becomes straightforwardness; guilt gives way to forgiveness; shame melts into freedom; and at last boredom is banished by the joy in living we never thought we deserved.

—Paula B., Arizona

(Books by Father Leo Booth include *The God Game: It's Your Move* and *Spirituality and Recovery*, available at www.fatherleo. com.)

The following articles were submitted by certified counselors or therapists for the *Women Helping Women* newsletter.

Why Counseling?

By Bonnie J. Benzies, PhD
(January 2004)

The information below is provided as a general overview only. Each individual, in consultation with family, friends, and GA members, must make decisions about her best recovery options.

First things first: The general rule is that if you have to choose between counseling and GA, especially early in recovery, go to GA. Either way, counseling can play a major role in recovery, for two reasons. It can help you identify and heal past wounds, and it can help you cope with the many consequences of your problem or compulsive gambling.

Examples of wounds from the past include: 1) abuse—physical, sexual, emotional, psychological; 2) developmental "holes" such as abandonment issues, inadequately developed coping and conflict resolution skills; 3) loss and grief that were never adequately pro-cessed; 4) repressed anger, guilt and/or shame; 5) cumulative stress from handling multiple demanding roles over extended periods of time; and 6) divorce and/or the "empty nest" in mid- or later life. Examples of more current issues, resulting from your gambling, in-clude: guilt, depression, family conflict/possibly divorce, legal prob-lems, unemployment, loss of children, isolation, fear, and shame.

Past wounding often predisposes women to gambling and oth-er addictions. Understanding these issues will help you know the "why" of your gambling and also ultimately free you from these unseen forces in the future. But, again, first things first: You need to begin with the present. And this will take some time, because by the time you have found GA you likely have left much damage in the wake of your gambling.

So what is the difference between counseling and GA? GA focuses mainly on external behavior: not gambling, one day at a time, by attending meetings; accepting the fellowship and support of others in the program; participating in Pressure Relief at the appropriate time; and learning to socialize in healthy, even helpful, ways. For most problem/compulsive gamblers, GA is the first doorway to recovery; its benefits are immeasurable—especially if you are able to find closed women's meetings.

However, because the issue of shame can be a significant barrier to women's recovery, GA is often not enough, especially early on. Some women will not get to GA unless they first do counseling to address the shame issues and receive needed encouragement to go to GA.

For those involved in GA, counseling focuses more on internal processes such as feelings, thoughts, and eventual insight into both past and present issues. While counseling can occur in a group format, many find individual sessions more helpful. For many women, individual counseling may be the first time they experience being the sole focus of a caring adult; it is also a place where they can learn again to trust and be trusted.

Ideally, you would attend both counseling and GA. To the extent your gambling behavior is managed via GA, counseling can focus on the many levels of personal healing which need to occur. If, however, you initially decide to only do counseling, it is critical that your counselor is highly skilled as an addictions counselor with expertise in problem/compulsive gambling. In this instance, your counselor must at least initially focus on your gambling behavior and its many consequences. Only when your gambling has stopped and you are solidly involved in GA can the counseling begin to focus on the "why" issues and your inner healing.

Another major difference between GA and counseling is that GA is free, while counseling can be quite costly. Thus, it makes good sense to utilize GA early in your recovery (Stage I Recovery) and then later, when finances have stabilized, begin counseling (Stage II Recovery). Again, the main exception to this is if you have been unable to get meaningfully involved in GA on your own.

(A licensed clinical psychologist and addictions specialist, Dr. Benzies serves on the board of directors of the Illinois Council on Problem and Compulsive Gambling. In addition to the private practice she has maintained for more than twenty years, she is the Director of Com

munity Psychology and facility MISA Coordinator at Elgin Mental Health Center.)

Issues Ignored—Problems Multiplied

By Mary Lou Costanzo, LCSW, NCGC
(January 2003)

Loneliness can eat away at your soul. Your children are gone, your husband is a bore—and maybe a boor, as well. Alcohol makes you hot and tired, instead of high. Pot is expensive, not to mention illegal. Other men are just as bad, or worse, than the one you have. What are you to do? Gamble?

Unfortunately, this is too often the case for many women who become problem gamblers. All of the ills described above can melt at the casino. You can get high without getting tired and sweaty from alcohol. You can feel exhilarated, cared for by others, and respected. And you can escape from your loneliness.

But this is all temporary, and the consequences of using gambling in this way are crippling. Losing all you have worked for, and even more sometimes, causes debilitating problems that develop very quickly and create many more issues than existed before.

What is profoundly difficult is that many women, when they start to gamble, do not realize the addictive potential of this activity until it is too late. In debt and overwhelmed, they then struggle with how to cope. This is where both Gamblers Anonymous and treatment come in.

Respect, concern, a feeling of caring and being cared for—all of these can return once a woman stops gambling and can visualize her life differently. Suddenly, "life begins at 50!" becomes possible.

Horizons can open up when recovery starts; a woman can change and her life can feel different—full. Change involves work though; recovery from pathological gambling is not easy. A gambler has to deal with issues she ignored before and has to struggle to resolve these issues without running away from the feelings they bring up. But the encouragement, support, and strength she gains through recovery enable her to deal with the problems and the feelings. She no longer feels the need to "run away" from the difficulties of her life, but feels able to face them and resolve them in the best ways she can.

(Nationally Certified Gambling Counselor Mary Lou Costanzo helps compulsive gamblers and their families through Connecticut's Problem Gambling Services.)

Are Depression and Problem Gambling Related?

By Mary Lou Costanzo, LCSW, NCGC
(February 2003)

To answer the above question correctly we probably need to break it down a little: Do people gamble too much because they are depressed, or does gambling too much cause depression? But we also need to ask other questions, the most important of which are: "What is depression anyway?" and "How is depression different from just feeling sad or down?"

Let's start with the last question first. Depression, as I discuss here, is different from feeling sad or down in several important ways. One way is duration. Other differences between sadness and depression relate to everyday activities, like eating and sleeping. Everyone has hours, days, sometimes even weeks of feeling low or "not right." Something bad happens, and the mood shifts to this state. But it goes away. It does not last long, and it does not result in a change in the person's overall functioning. With passing sadness, work or school still gets handled, sleep remains undisturbed, and eating is stable.

If this state continues, though, or if it worsens over time, it can evolve into a state of clinical depression. Years ago, when I was first starting out as a clinical social worker, someone suggested a pneumonic to help remember the signs and symptoms of depression: SIG E. CAPS. Pretend this is a name and go from there:

S—Has *sleep* been disturbed—trouble getting to sleep/staying asleep or waking very early (the most common sleep disturbance of depression)?

I—Has there been a change in *initiative* or has the person lost interest in usual activities?

G—Has there been excessive *guilt* over actions or events?

E—Has the person lost all or most *energy*?

C—Has *concentration* been difficult?

A—Has there been an *appetite* change, either increased or decreased?

P—Has the person had more *physical complaints* than usual, such as headaches?

S—Has the person thought about or acted on *suicide ideas?*

Now that we have criteria to differentiate between a "normal" feeling of sadness and clinical depression, we can move on to the original question. Is depression related to problem gambling? The answer is yes, both as cause and effect.

A person suffering with undiagnosed depression will do almost anything to feel better. Depression is often left untreated by the sufferer, who may be afraid of psychiatry and/or medication. Unfortunately, this lack of professional treatment can result in self-medication. When compared with the antidepressants available on the market, self-medication is not nearly as effective and is sometimes addicting. So self-medicating with gambling may help you feel better, but once you stop, the symptoms return. This scenario illustrates depression as a *cause* of problem gambling.

Likewise, any behavior that is addictive and/or self-destructive can result in symptoms of depression. It is clear from research into depression in the past twenty years that the brain changes are the same whether someone has a "predisposition" (i.e. inherited inclination) to depression, or whether something happens in a person's life that causes upset. The chemicals are not in balance and symptoms occur. So, if gambling too much gets you into financial, legal, or other trouble, causing emotional upset, you can become clinically depressed. In such a case, depression is the *effect* of problem gambling.

Either way, there is treatment. The new categories of medications are safe, non-addicting and incredibly effective and have literally been a lifesaver for many. They are not to be feared! And psychotherapy, in combination with medication, has been shown to be the most effective treatment for symptoms of clinical depression.

Brain Drain

Diane Rae Davis, PhD, Washington
(July 2000)

Ever wonder why it is so doggone hard to quit gambling compulsively? And stay quit? Recent research shows some indications that compulsive gambling may "hijack" the reward and pleasure pathways of the brain in the same way as drug addiction.

For example, according to Dr. Carl Erickson at the University of Texas College of Pharmacy, using cocaine triggers floods of dopamine in the brain (this is your brain on coke!). After enough time, your brain will adapt to this situation by cutting down on your own internal "natural" dopamine by reducing the number of receptors available. After this adaptation, without cocaine, you feel bad, depressed, nothing looks or feels good, and craving sets in. The only way to get back to normal is more cocaine. And so it goes. To make matters even worse, your brain has also stored "privileged" memories of the intense pleasure you got from the cocaine high. This memory is forever and will take precedence in affecting your emotions and behavior.

Research using new brain imaging techniques, cited in the National Research Council's report, indicates that gambling and drug abuse may share the same addictive process and have similar effects in the brain. For example, winning was found to induce the same euphoria as that produced by psychoactive drugs; brain dopamine levels were found to be elevated while research subjects played a video game for money.

Genetic scientists have found molecular evidence that suggests a similar genetic pathway between compulsive gambling and drug addiction. Although the very few studies on compulsive gambling and the brain are preliminary, evidence is accumulating that compulsive gambling involves the same mechanisms and brain adaptations involved in drug addiction.

What might this mean to the woman who is struggling to quit gambling or maintain her recovery? If the same brain adaptations are occurring as in drug abuse, we could learn some things from the drug addiction school of hard knocks. First, it's important to forgive yourself for wanting to gamble, craving to gamble, and even relapsing into gambling. It takes weeks, months, even years for the brain to readapt to its normal way of functioning. The "privileged" memories last a lifetime.

Second, there is speculation among some researchers that "talk therapy" and twelve-step meetings can actually help change the brain in a positive direction. "Keep coming back, it works!" makes even more sense.

Third, remember that you are not "recovered," but "recovering." You may never rid yourself of some intense memories, so it's important to work your recovery program every day, one day at a time....

Spirituality: Definition? Not Required!

By Joanna Franklin MS, NCGC II
(September 2002)

Much of the following information comes, not from me, but through me. It comes from my teachers and mentors on the subject, with my gratitude for their patience and endless encouragement. Lori Rugle, PhD, Joe Ciarrocchi, PhD, Deb Haskins, PhD, and Jim Walsh, PhD. Though they are all PhDs, I don't hold it against them...often.

"The time has come the walrus said to speak of many things, of ships and sails and sealing wax, of cabbages and kings." So goes an introduction to Lewis Carroll's *Alice in Wonderland,* as she begins another adventure through the looking glass.

The time also has come to speak of many things when we look at spirituality and recovery. In this era of aroma therapy and crystals, getting a good grasp on spirituality and the role it should play in one's personal recovery can be confusing, if not outright difficult. Spirituality can be defined so many ways I would take up the remainder of this article quoting the top ten definitions. Many wonderful authors have written to the subject far more eloquently than I ever could. At the end of these notes I will list just a few of my many favorites for interested readers.

As an outsider who has attended GA meetings since 1979, I have noted in many states around the U.S.—as others have—that GA has made an effort to secularize their twelve steps. Unlike AA's steps, from which GA adapted the twelve steps in 1957, GA's steps somewhat de-emphasize the importance of a "spiritual awakening" as part of recovery. Perhaps the common confusion between religion and spirituality affected the issue. In my view, while a person can nurture, or even implant, spirituality within the context of a traditional religion or faith practice, a traditional religion certainly is not a prerequisite for a full spiritual life.

Let me suggest to the reader, as Dr. Rugle presents it, spirituality can be your ethical practice, your value system, that little voice in your head that says, "No, don't do that," as well as an element of a religion. My work with compulsive gamblers has shown me many patterns of thought and behavior. One pattern has more than one compulsive gambler, often relatively new to recovery, telling me about dismissing the practice of their childhood religion. Often it is around the adolescent years, "…when my parents stopped making me go to church." Sometimes it is after a significant loss, death, or other hardship, and the gambler clearly expresses her or his anger toward this "mean" God who let this horrible thing happen.

Also clear to me is the missing element, as the search for serenity continues. Debts get paid, meetings attended, gambling stopped, but sometimes something is still missing inside. Perhaps the need to reconcile with one's faith is part of the answer. Pastoral counselors are well-trained in this service. Perhaps the need to explore the topic will bring the searcher to some answers that suit the adult ready to practice a faith that fits. Perhaps the quest that lasts a lifetime can begin with a prayer from another colleague, Chris Anderson, whose presentations speak of the recovering compulsive gambler reaching out to pray in the simplest—the most direct—of ways. Consider beginning your day with "help" or "help me today" and end your day with the words "thank you."

In my mind this central connection is indeed part of Steps 2 and 3, and the rest all comes as we are ready for it.

References: A wonderful book on the topic is The Road Less Traveled *by Scott Peck, and a book focused on gambling is* Luck: A Secular Faith *by Wayne E. Oates. Many writings of Father Leo Booth [an ACOG (Adult Children of Gamblers)] address the topic beautifully, as do some writings by Rabbi Twerski, such as:* When Do the Good Things Start; Waking Up Just In Time *and* That's Not Fault, It's a Character Trait. *Rabbi Twerski's* The Spiritual Self, *written with Charles Schultz of "Peanuts" fame, applies well. Of course, the "One Day at a Time" and "Easy Does It" books are some of the many on affirmations helping us all change—one day at a time.*

Defining Recovery, Part I

By Joanna Franklin, MS, NCGC II
(June 2005)

The word recovery has more definitions than I can count. Every time I think I have just the right "new" definition for recovery, I hear a newer one from someone who shares from personal experience. Recovery for the main road women in Gamblers Anonymous includes the comfort of support from those with the same concerns: the relief that comes from identification and understanding you are not alone, "that woman just told *my* story and that one too."

GA has come to represent so many elements of recovery it is easy to think this must be the best way to find, to work, and [to] enjoy real recovery. In 1979, when I began working with gamblers and their families, we were the first state that funded [a] treatment program for gamblers. We saw women present for care for the first time. (The only other gambling treatment program, in Brecksville, Ohio, was for veterans.)

We saw teens and we saw people from other cultures. We saw lots of gambling problems that seemed very much the same. "I have lost all or almost all of my money, behind on the bills, family is angry/hurt, has left or is about to leave. I may be arrested, may lose my job and my home...." The problems were so similar from one gambler to the next we mistakenly thought that we could help all our clients with the same package of tools.

First, we would assess and get a good clear picture of all the problems, prioritize what to do first, second, and third, and then get the gambler to a GA meeting and the family to GamAnon. We would offer support, understanding, acceptance, problem solving, and solutions to the reality issues one step at a time, as they worked the twelve steps one day at a time. Well, who could ask for more? It sounds simple and straightforward enough. Clearly a system that works and works well for those who take advantage of the structure of and help available in the program.

That would have been the beginning and end of creative clinical care for gamblers and their families, but for a handful of women gamblers who said no. "No? What do you mean, no?" "I don't want to go to those meetings." We, in fact, found many women who were more than uncomfortable in the male-dominated GA meetings in our area. We had only two meetings in the area and no women attending way back then. I pushed, I urged, I prodded, I encouraged, I ordered, I pleaded, I tried to "sell" the idea of going to a meeting as best I could; and though many did try meetings, many did not.

In the next issue of WHW (August 2005), Joanna will share about the solutions she and her colleagues developed for this "new kind of client."

Defining Recovery, Part 2

By Joanna Franklin, MS, NCGC II
(August 2005)

Joanna Franklin and other gambling treatment professionals discovered some twenty-five years ago that the Gamblers Anonymous meetings of that era simply couldn't help many women into recovery

from compulsive gambling. This knowledge prompted them to develop
new treatment solutions.

When I was introduced to a different kind of client, I found something new I could try that turned out to be very helpful. I just listened to what she was saying to me. Many of these women clients were abuse survivors and very uncomfortable around males, because they were reminded of the abuse. They did not enjoy meetings; they did not relate [to] or identify with the men at those meetings; and they did not get anything helpful from the efforts the men made to help them with recovery.

We counselors learned that recovery is defined by each individual who is searching for her or his very own road. Some recovering problem gamblers take a road less traveled that does not include going to GA. For many there just isn't any GA in their area, or they cannot get to the local meetings for a variety of reasons.

As a counselor I have learned not to define for my clients how they should live their lives. My job isn't to tell them how to recover, but rather to help them find their own way to their own goals. I have learned to be open-minded enough to accept with care and respect every woman's efforts to heal and recover as she sees fit. My role is to help.

So many folks use GA, finding everything they need there to do very well. GA members are a gift and a blessing for the others who come into the program and learn how to recover using those great twelve steps AA pioneered. But many do not use those meetings. Sometimes they use different meetings, sometimes no meetings. But they can still recover. Oh yes, they can absolutely still recover.

The research calls it natural recovery. They find their road and set their goals. Some see their counselors, perhaps return to school, get more active in their church, join a survivors group, a grief group, or just read more and talk to friends and family.

The best lesson twenty-five years of treating gamblers has taught me is that there is no one definition of recovery. Recovery is discovery of what a woman wants to be, what she does not want to be, and the glory and power and joy we all have in us when we find and embrace change, not as a goal but as a process. Turns out there are dozens of ways to take twelve steps, hundreds of words for recovery, and as many roads as there are women to walk them.

Today, I am much less arrogant about thinking I know what is best for everyone. Turns out each of us has in our hearts all our own answers and the right way to go on the right road. We are not all mothers and not all of us should be. We do not all have jobs outside of the home and not all of us should.

We do not all go to churches, temple, or services; we do not all wear the same size; we do not all have loving partners, or understanding families or forgiving friends. But we can all have recovery, and we can have it our way—with GA or not, with a counselor or not, with a Higher Power or not—but we do it one day at a time.

For many, perhaps, recovery is being happy and safe, or sober and sane, at peace, solvent, loving and loved, or forgiving and forgiven, as the prayer says. One day at a time for all the rest of our days, we define recovery for ourselves and share with each other to encourage the search, work, and discovery of each individual's personal recovery.

Don't Shame Yourself Out of Recovery

Mary Gilmore, RN, CCGC

The most striking benefit of treatment for compulsive gambling is recovery. Treatment works! In focusing on women who are compulsive gamblers, it may be most appropriate for women to ask, "Why shouldn't I get treatment?" After all, it is 1999 and when professional treatment is available for someone who is suffering, why not take advantage of it?

One of the main reasons women avoid treatment is shame. The word shame has many meanings. For instance, many of us felt shame when we returned to our senses after a period of abstinence from gambling. The lies we told, the dishonesty we practiced, the irresponsibility.... Understandably, our behavior while gambling compulsively often created shame, but our program teaches us how to forgive ourselves.

A much more destructive type of shame can keep us from

seeking help. This is the "toxic" shame that John Bradshaw and other mental health professionals have written about. Shame can sentence a woman to a lifetime of self-condemnation and misery. Shame that may very well not even be valid! Or shame that may rightfully belong to someone else. Shame that frequently makes women feel they "should have known better," or that they "don't deserve help."

Shame! It can be one of the "best" reasons for relapse. Treatment to reduce or eradicate shame is helpful. Self-help books on shame can be beneficial; of course, some women feel they don't deserve to have a decrease in shame. A woman's dawning belief that she deserves recovery is another benefit of treatment.

Women often need to have some assistance in learning and accepting that compulsive gambling is an illness. Women compulsive gamblers are sick, not bad. The behaviors that occur during active compulsive gambling are often inappropriate, but once the woman stops gambling, the inappropriate behaviors usually begin to disappear.

It is very important to use the intellect, versus feelings, in order to get help. The shameful feelings are all part of the illness, so making an intellectual decision is often necessary. More feelings will come along later.

Many times people will say it is a "cop out" to view compulsive gambling as an illness—that the gambler *should* feel shame. "Good guilt" when a person does something wrong motivates the person to avoid wrong behaviors. However, shame can be so overwhelming that it works just the opposite. Often shame is so painful that the woman wants to gamble more than ever to escape the negative self-image generated by shame.

If you can view this toxic shame as an old, moldy buffalo hide, a desire to escape makes a lot of sense. On the other hand, if someone likes the old hide, she might have other problems in addition to compulsive gambling. Professional treatment is available and the female compulsive gambler of 1999 can get treatment and is deserving of help. Rather than returning to the behaviors that create more shame and continuing in the vicious cycle, it makes sense to get help.

Yes! We Can Help Each Other

Bobbe McGinley, MA, NCGC, Clinical Director
(January 2000)

As an addiction treatment professional, I have frequently witnessed the pain women have suffered as a result of gambling addiction. Their history verifies their pain, with losses of self-esteem, family, and friends. Major consequences, such as loss of employment, homes, and marriages, are also part of gambling women's pain. For each woman, it is her nightmare, and she will need to process it over time, in order to overcome. Women can reach a plateau of self-awareness, and eventually even forgiveness, through the love and care of other recovering women.

More and more women are becoming mesmerized by gambling at machines. And more are beginning to recognize their problem—some before life's tragedies strike. In my experience, we owe this earlier awareness to the outreach and advocacy of women who have gone before. Women sharing their experience, strength, and hope will always be a primary adjunct to another woman gambler coming to grips with the reality of her addiction. I frequently mention the courage of recovering women I know when a new client comes to me feeling hopeless and out of control.

I give my clients a list of Gamblers Anonymous meetings. Many compulsive gamblers initially respond to the idea of meetings with trepidation, and this applies to both genders, not just women. I can certainly relate to the fear of sharing in a group setting. "Will I be accepted or merely tolerated? Will the group perceive my ignorance of the problem and of the group process as lack of motivation, or perhaps denial? Will the group hear me as an individual, or might the members assess me as not having hit bottom yet and turn me out? Will they be compassionate and understand how the suffering tears at my soul?" These and countless other questions confront women initially seeking help with their gambling. The questions are part of the reason why women need, and are such strong support for, other women.

Life cycles produce major events, which sometimes are stressful and draw some to gambling. At first, they perceive it as an innocent and safe way to pass some time. Divorce, retirement, loss of a loved one—these and other events may provide another area of common ground. Women can take advantage of these similarities. I encourage women to continue to reach out to each other, to educate themselves about the addiction, and to utilize community resources.

The personal progress I have witnessed as women work on recovery fosters the hope I am sharing here. Those women have been and continue to be an inspiration.

Understand Yourself

Bobbe McGinley, MA, NCGC, Clinical Director
(November 2000)

Rather than give in to any power of your addiction that you wake up with in the morning, treat yourself to an impartial piece of paper and bold ink pen instead. Anxiety, fear, anger, resentment, insecurities: all are feelings attempting to tell you something. Feelings try to get your attention in order to help you understand yourself better, to really know who you are and what you are about.

For the most part, many of us do our best to stay away from uncomfortable feelings. We seek ways to ignore ourselves and the life predicaments we get ourselves into. Thus, our addiction of choice becomes a mirage to relieve our anxieties. The mirage calls to us to follow it into the void of nothingness, where no person or thing exists except emptiness itself. If, before we succumb to the mirage, we stop for a moment and check in with our most intimate thoughts and feelings, we can discover more about ourselves. One area in which we may come to understand ourselves better is intimacy.

Intimacy is often misunderstood. Our society has sexualized it. Thus, in common language we ask, "Have you been intimate yet?" implying, "Have you had sex yet?" Most of us have had sexual experiences looking for intimacy, but ended up feeling empty instead.

True intimacy is first to know yourself. Who are you? What is this fear or that fear about? Why, after so much work on yourself, do you still feel insecure and depressed? When are you ever going to stop being jealous? Writing out these personal and private thoughts helps get the clutter out of your head. You have better self-understanding because you've looked at yourself in ways you've never looked before. Seeing these feelings for what they are motivates you to take action regarding them. Writing about your feelings allows you the opportunity to run toward yourself rather than away from yourself. Among other benefits, keeping a journal helps you confront your addiction.

You know that your addiction is a disease. It generates resistance to personal intimate feelings. The disease prefers to activate itself in your system rather than allow you to face all that angst you woke up with this morning. So, as part of your lifetime recovery process, why not make facing your feelings through the art of journal writing a daily tool to assist you in holding on to your internal community, the intimate self?

You are the most important component of your recovery. Take yourself seriously. Listen to your private, intimate feelings. Allow yourself the luxury of time and reflection to maintain your commitment to fully live your life.

Conscious Contact: Brain, Mind, and Addiction, Part 1 of 2

Lori Rugle, PhD
(September 2003)

Much research today, funded by national organizations, is focusing on the neurobiology of addiction. The catch phrase is "addiction is a brain disease." This line of research has served to help "legitimize" the field of addiction. Research is showing that alcoholism, drug addiction, and compulsive gambling—my particular area of focus—have genetic and biological bases. These addictions are not just self-centered, immoral, bad behavior.

If addiction is a brain disease, what is the brain? Basically, it is an organ like other organs in the body—heart, liver, kidneys.... The brain is made up of tissue, blood cells, and nerve cells. This collection of nerve cells differentiates the brain from other organs. We can think of the brain as a bio-organic computer. Its nerve cells work through transmission of biochemical signals that create bio-electric impulses. The chemicals responsible for transmission of messages from one nerve cell to another are called neurotransmitters.

Three of the neurotransmitters most significant in addictive disorders are dopamine, serotonin, and norepinephrine. Dopamine and a system of nerve cells responsive to it have been identified as the primary reward system in the brain. This system appears to manage feelings of pleasure and satisfaction and also controls how we respond to reward and punishment. The dopamine system also affects memory and learning, since we tend to remember what is pleasurable or satisfying. We can trigger the system's actions over and over, trying to learn from what is rewarding or punishing or painful. Many addictive substances and activities directly impact on this system by mimicking the action of dopamine or increasing the release of dopamine into the nervous system.

Serotonin largely manages the emotional system. A lack of serotonin or of the ability of the nervous system to process this neurotransmitter contributes to depression, emotional instability, and impulsive behavior.

The third neurotransmitter discussed here works on the arousal system. Norepinephrine is the "fight or flight" agent, managing alertness, attention, and responses to potentially dangerous, stressful, anxiety-provoking situations.

Scientific studies increasingly demonstrate differences between these major brain systems in individuals who develop addictive disorders and those who do not. Such differences have been shown to be, not simply a result of using toxic substances that can damage the brain but, genetically mediated differences that existed prior to the addiction and contribute to a person's higher risk for addiction.

Individuals who are more biologically at risk for addiction are likely to have a neurobiological basis for deficits in experiencing pleasure, reward, and satisfaction. Additionally, they are more likely to be emotionally unstable and impulsive, or experience either over- or under-arousal.

Addictive substances and behaviors act in some ways to "fix" such neurobiological risk factors. However, the addictive "cure" only serves to intensify the problem, by further aggravating the underlying biological problems.

Taken alone, this discussion of addiction in relation to the biology of the brain probably seems disheartening. But the mind is a component of the addiction equation, as well, and next month I'll discuss tools for reducing our subservience to the brain's neurotransmitter systems.

Conscious Contact: Brain, Mind, and Addiction, Part 2 of 2

By Lori Rugle, PhD
(October 2003)

Last month we learned that the brain may be somewhat of a "villain" when it comes to addiction. The addiction equation also contains an element that can play the "hero": the mind. Certainly our physical brains set the baseline for mind. However, mind seems to have a choice in how it responds to the physiological boundaries established by our brains.

In addition to the results I spoke of previously, research studies are making it clear that other risk factors contribute. While genetic, neurobiological factors exist, they are not the only—perhaps not even the most significant—factors that place some of us at risk for developing addictions. Biological factors may provide less than 25 percent of the explanation for why one person becomes addicted and another doesn't. Clearly, other critical factors demand attention in order to understand the cause of addictive behaviors.

The brain can be touched and measured. With modern neuro-imaging techniques, we can even see pictures of the brain as it works.

What, however, is the mind? Where is it located? Does the mind "exist" in the brain? Is it only the sum of the brain's neurochemical impulses, or is it something more? I recently asked participants in a workshop I was facilitating to define "mind."

After a significant silence, people talked about mind consisting of thoughts, ideas, memories, experiences, learning, images, feelings, beliefs. Then I asked, "If we took all of our thoughts, memories, experiences, feelings and just added them all up, would the sum of all these things equal 'mind,' or would there still be something more?" Everyone agreed that we would also have to include our spirit, something that makes us unique and at the same time ties us all together.

These questions about mind are questions that scientists, philosophers, and clergy have been debating for centuries. Our minds do make choices. We can choose meditation or prayer to manage sadness, anger, fear, and loneliness; or we can chose to drink, drug, shop, eat, or gamble, trying to numb out these feelings. We can choose to exercise to help reduce stress, focus our attention, and manage our feelings. We can use our minds to learn to accept the limitations of our brains and our bodies, and to learn loving and compassionate ways to manage our impulses, express our feelings, and cope with stress and problems.

For some, making such healthy choices is extremely difficult, because the biology of their brains works against them. These individuals may suffer from severe depression, attention deficit disorder, manic-depression, or disorders of impulse control. Certainly, to reduce the risk of using addictive substances or behaviors to self-medicate, the compassionate choice for some individuals may be appropriate medication.

However, it is important to recognize that medication helps the brain to function. While this may assist an individual to better utilize the mind, medication does not necessarily "heal" the mind or, by itself, stop addictive behavior. Ideally, the mind will be used to make healthy choices, not choosing to seek escape, euphoria, or relief via the quick fix of addiction.

At the same workshop I mentioned earlier, we also talked about how we can change the chemistry of our brains through activities such as relaxation, prayer, meditation, eating mindfully, exercising, and such. When you take a few minutes to breathe deeply and slowly, your brain chemistry automatically changes, your brain waves change.

One person suggested that when a compulsive gambler is gambling she or he changes the brain in the same way, since many gamblers report that gambling relaxes them. While this may seem true on the surface, gambling and other addictive behaviors only provide the illusion of providing this type of relief. If we took a brain image of someone who was gambling and compared it to someone who was meditating, we would have vastly different pictures.

Addiction is about mindlessness; conversely, meditation, prayer, and relaxation are about mindfulness. Addiction is about forgetting who we are, and meditation is about remembering who we really are. About remembering that, when our true minds are "enabled," the elements in the addiction equation are greater than the sum of their parts; each mind is a spark of a higher mind and a greater reality. If we accept our biology and use our minds to maintain this conscious contact, we can live mindfully, not turning to the illusory safety of addiction.

(Lori Rugle, PhD. of Trimeridian, Inc., in Indianapolis, Indiana, specializes in treating and understanding compulsive gambling.)

Boundaries

By Carol Stamos, MC, CPC, NCC, Phoenix, Arizona
(August 2000)

Boundaries can be defined as a distance placed between self and another person, place, or thing. They help us to have a sense of separateness, to know where we end and others begin. Healthy boundaries provide a sense of empowerment. We know who we are and are not, what we believe and do not believe, and what we think, feel, and want.

How many of us have ever asked ourselves, "Who am I?" People with healthy boundaries have a clear sense of themselves. They are secure within themselves. They know how to assert themselves in an appropriate manner so as to avoid the role of victim. Learning to say "no" is often difficult, especially for women who have been socialized to believe that they must care for, care about, and please others. Many fear that to verbalize and/or act upon their own needs and wants will be perceived as "selfish." This denial of self, over the long term, eventually results in sense of shame, decreased self-esteem, aggression, and inappropriate acting out of repressed thoughts and feelings.

Poor boundary setting is typically learned behavior of dysfunctional families in which parenting skills are weak or nonexistent. Rules and limits are too strict or lacking. Traumatic experiences in the form of abuse, addictions, illness, death, divorce, poverty, crime, and being rescued from consequences of one's own behavior often result in inappropriate childhood boundary development. Dysfunctional family settings become arenas that promote lack of individuation of self and development of family secrets and sense of shame.

One's relationships, spirituality, physical, sexual, and emotional being are impacted by boundary development. Resolution of issues in these areas of our life enhances personal growth and increased self-esteem. Appropriate grieving of past losses, and letting go of anger and resentments for past hurts, is at the root of the healing process. Unhealthy boundaries are a result of learned behavior. With time and perseverance, they can be unlearned and replaced with healthy boundaries.

Following development and maintenance of real self through supportive relationships is key. Some steps that can assist in establishing healthy boundaries through honesty and responsibility are as follows:

- Group participation, discussion, and skill practice in a safe environment of truth and accountability.

- Acceptance of responsibility for what we allow for ourselves and for others by learning that we have the power to say "no" in fairness to ourselves and to maintain respect in fairness to others.

- Work the Twelve Steps of Recovery.

- Journal daily on our thoughts, feelings, and incidents of daily maintenance and violations of boundary setting. Development of healthy boundaries affords us the opportunity to be true to ourselves and to others with confidence, thereby enhancing recovery and personal growth.

11

Today

Two days before my sixty-fifth birthday, I made an appointment to visit the Social Security office and apply for benefits. Because the Social Security check would be extra income, I decided to put 90 percent of the check into a retirement plan to save for a home. I was informed that I could borrow money on my retirement plan for the purchase of a home. I also saved money by shopping at thrift stores and yard sales and I carried a peanut butter sandwich and an apple to work each day. In the year 2000, I finally had enough equity in my retirement plan and applied for a loan for a down payment on a house. After checking the real estate listings on my computer, I found six properties in a senior citizen community. My realtor drove me around Sun City, population 37,000, and I found the perfect house. The community covers approximately thirteen square miles, and residents share seven recreation centers with swimming pools, seven golf courses, a library, shopping centers, dancing, crafts, and enough to keep me busy for the rest of my life.

I've now lived in Sun City for five years and spend my time gardening, enjoy photography, dancing, working on the computer, and going on occasional dinner dates. My health is great, and I still have a sense of humor.

Some incidents in life can't be discharged with humor. I learned from an unpleasant experience that I couldn't share my past with everyone. I dated a man for a couple of months and decided I'd confess all to him. It was not an easy task. One night while my friend and I sat in the kitchen, I said, "Tomorrow night I'm driving down to the Perryville prison to start a GA meeting."

He asked, "Why are you going to a prison to start a meeting?"

"Because I'm a compulsive gambler, and there may be women in there that need to know the warning signs to becoming a compulsive gambler."

"Well, why would you go to a prison?"

"Because I was in prison ten years ago."

"What!"

"I was sent to prison ten years ago for embezzling money to gamble with."

"My God! You sure know how to drop a bomb!"

"But remember, that was ten years ago, and my life has changed."

"Yes, but prison...." And that was the end of the romance.

I am dating a gentleman today who knows of my past and treats me with the greatest respect.

I'm grateful that my family has always supported me and loved me. My grandson, Tyler, is twenty-one now, a handsome six-foot-tall young man, studying to be an attorney. Tyler never tried drugs or alcohol and doesn't smoke. His mom, Juannie, is free from drugs and alcohol—one day at a time—and works as an RN.

Chelsea, my granddaughter, is now twenty-eight years old and is a licensed CNA and is considering further education in the nursing program. She bought a home with a pool, has a wonderful man in her life, and two darling children, Brandon, who is in fourth grade, and Corinne, who is four, going on ten. Chelsea never tried drugs or alcohol and doesn't smoke.

Damian, my grandson, is twenty-nine and has a lively four-year-old son, Drake. Damian could have been a great baseball player, but when we moved to Phoenix he stopped playing baseball. Shortly after quitting baseball, he began to skip school and joined a gang of boys and started using drugs. Damian is in jail now, awaiting trial for stealing a truck and running from the police. We pray for him.

Kathy, my oldest daughter, has a heart problem, which medication is keeping under control. After her boyfriend died two years ago, she moved in with me. She's currently waiting for a biopsy to see if she has breast cancer.

Bev, my middle daughter, has more then a year free from drugs and alcohol. If she follows her program, she will have her RN license back soon.

Juanita, my youngest daughter, is sober and clean and is also an RN.

My son Gerry is married to a lovely gal, lives in a beautiful home, has two grandchildren, and is a successful entrepreneur.

I will always believe in my family and love them, even when they don't believe in themselves.

Betty, my AA sponsor and dearest friend, died in Bert's arms after a long illness. I can close my eyes and still hear her voice quoting parts of our twelve-step program.

Ace died of old age and went to doggie heaven. Two of the Pomeranians we brought from Yuma died in fights with larger dogs.

After four years of recovery, the GA members in Phoenix elected me as trustee for the Arizona and New Mexico areas. At that time, there were approximately 128 trustees from around the United States, and less than a dozen were women. Other GA members joined me in traveling around the state to open new meetings. It was a great opportunity to learn how the GA program worked.

I am fortunate to have found a part-time job in a lovely church near my home. The priest is a wonderful man and is aware of my past. Working with the priest and the parishioners has enhanced my spirituality. Each religious holiday, plants are purchased to decorate the altar, and when the holidays pass and the plants need more care, the women from the church donate the lilies, chrysanthemums, and poinsettias to my garden. Special rays of sunshine and my green thumb have created an oasis in my backyard. I don't wear prison jeans anymore, but I do slip on jeans to work with my flowers. I know that I want to be here for the rest of my life.

Each night I thank God that there was a twelve-step program for me to follow when I stopped gambling, and I didn't have to go out and discover one. Because of this program, I have more than fifteen years free from gambling. By listening to therapy from other recovering gamblers and by applying the principles of the program, I found my inner strength (spirituality) that we're all born with. This strength has enhanced my connection to others and to my Higher Power. Today, there's no limit to what I can do. The only limits are the ones I put on myself. I no longer have to give up my dreams; I just have to be sure they're realistic dreams.

After completing seven years of probation, I returned to the Perryville prison to start a GA meeting for inmates. It took an additional year for the paperwork and interviews to be completed before they allowed me back into the Perryville facility.

In April 1999, the *Women Helping Women* newsletter was started as a local information sheet for the Phoenix area. With the help of a couple of GA friends, it evolved into a worldwide letter. A female gambler from Tucson volunteered to upload the newsletter onto the Internet. She told us that in a few short months, we heard from Nova Scotia, Australia, Japan, Newfoundland, Montreal, Austria, and England, and all across the United States. Since that time we have also heard from readers in Iceland, Ireland, South Africa, Poland, and Guatemala. The *Women Helping Women* newsletter is in its seventh year of publication. The following words were printed on the front page of the initial newsletter: "The purpose of this letter is to fill a need for sharing, connecting, and supporting the women who are in recovery from a gambling addiction."

We've received e-mails from faraway places where gambling is available: a gal from Australia who couldn't find another compulsive gambler in her area; a woman living on an island near Japan who had gambling close by and said no one on the island wanted to stop gambling and no counselors had been trained to treat compulsive gamblers; a woman who lived on a remote Native American reservation and tried to start a meeting a year ago and is still waiting for other compulsive gamblers to join her; and a lonely gal from Alaska who couldn't find another compulsive gambler. I've been corresponding with compulsive gamblers who are incarcerated for crimes they committed to feed their addiction. This is my way of giving back to the GA program.

My computer program has a feature that records the number of hits our newsletter receives, and it reports between three hundred and five hundred hits a day. Three years after the newsletter established its name on the Internet, we added a WHW Email Network. Recovering female gamblers can send emails to each other through the network. It has a membership of about a hundred women. A GA sister from South Carolina assumed the responsibility for coordinating members' information and introducing new women to our network group.

I have experienced many changes in my years of recovery, but some routines are difficult to modify. It's been thirty years since my husband, Wally, died and fifteen years since my mom, my son Graham, and my friend Tommie died, and each night before I kneel down to say my prayers, I kiss their pictures good night. Each year I say this will the *last* year, but I guess the *last* year hasn't come yet. Perhaps that's because, traditionally, women have been caretakers for the family, and it is difficult for us to break these traditions. Many women are born with a maternal instinct, which dictates our actions and can put us in codependent situations. By applying the principle of "tough love" and "letting go," we learn to break this practice. When I'm pleasing everyone, I please no one. Sometimes I'm eager to please others to avoid conflict.

Approximately twelve years after my release from prison, I attended a conference on gambling issues, and many of the attendees were professionals in areas of problem gambling. I recognized the name of one of the gentlemen at the conference and asked my friend Don Hulen if the man might be related to my victim. He said, "Go talk to him and ask him." Twelve years earlier, the judge had given me an order that I was not to contact my victim.

So on rubbery legs I walked over to him and said, "Do you remember about twelve years ago when a secretary from your company in Yuma embezzled a lot of money?"

"Why yes, I do remember," he answered.

"Well, I'm the secretary."

His smile faded and I waited for him to splash coffee in my face from the cup he was carrying. To my surprise, he seemed to understand.

"Oh my goodness! Did you ever have to go to prison?"

"Yes, the judge sentenced me to two years."

"I'm sorry to hear that." He shared a story with me about his family and their decision to sell all their properties because of illness in the family. I was grateful to have the opportunity to apologize and asked him to pass my apology on to his family.

I have learned to forgive myself for the crime I committed. I can't run away from my past, because every corner I turn, here I am.

I know that it's important to take care of myself and be aware of my limitations. What might begin as loneliness, fatigue, or depression, can result in a domino effect. First, I become depressed and then lonely and tired. Then I'm tired and I forgot why I was depressed. Maybe I was hungry, so I eat, and when I'm confused, I tend to overeat. If I become angry and forget why I'm angry, I add the problem of guilt. It's like trying to catch falling dominos. This is the part where I have to stop and take care of me.

When I walked into my first twelve-step meeting, I felt unworthy and thought no one understood me. What I found was love and support. I also found that sympathy—"You poor thing"—is a dangerous commodity, because it encourages a person to feel like the victim and stay in their pain. Empathy is fine and lets the person know we understand their pain. I'm not writing this story to educate the world about compulsive gambling or to shape your opinion on casinos or Internet gambling, but instead to carry a message to other compulsive gamblers on how to stop gambling.

I hope this book brings some awareness to those who read it. I've written what I've experienced, heard at meetings, and read in newspapers or magazines.

I didn't wake up one morning and say, "Gee, I think I'll become a compulsive gambler." I don't know why I became a compulsive gambler, but I'm grateful I found a way to stop, and I discovered that stopping gambling would not be enough. A friend suggested I look at my character defects and begin to make some changes. My understanding was that, "If everyone around me did the things they were supposed to do, I wouldn't have to do the things I am doing." It was as simple as that.

As my recovery progressed, I learned how to work the steps—"One day at a time"—to find a sponsor, to seek a Higher Power, and to listen. I have learned how to give back to the program what the program has given to me.

The painful wounds and memories of my gambling have started to heal, and I'm building a new life. At the age of seventy-six, I've learned to laugh and enjoy life once more, and I have faith. I may not have everything I want today, but I have everything I need, and there's balance in my life, emotionally, physically, and spiritually.

I'm aware that I'm just one bet away from another disaster, so I stay close to the program and other GA members. Today I have a positive attitude and more openness, self-motivation, and responsibility. I know that if I ever go out and gamble again, there's no guarantee that I would ever have another desire to stop. At this time in my life, I live alone, and I'm happy as I walk through my little home. I thank God for helping me climb out of the mess I created. No one in my family has followed my gambling addiction…yet. GA is not my whole life, but GA makes my life whole.

Gambling will never just go away, but we can learn to live with it. It's available on the computer now, so no one has to leave their home to gamble. With the number of Native American casinos opening around the country, gambling is in everyone's backyard. I just read a book about gambling in the early days of the Wild West, and it described how the Indians gambled away their ponies, tepees, and wives, long before the cowboys came along. The Bible tells us that more than two thousand years ago, Roman soldiers sat beneath the cross where Jesus was being crucified and drew lots for his garments. Governments depend on gambling revenues. Churches and other groups like the Elks, VFW, etc. depend on bingo for fund-raisers.

A *compulsive* gambler can never gamble normally, but we don't have to gamble if we don't want to. There are ways to stop. Several programs are available to give the compulsive gambler support such as: the Gamblers Anonymous twelve-step program; professional counseling; GamBlock, a computer program which blocks problem gamblers from accessing Internet gambling sites; and a self-exclusion program where the gambler can be added to a list of people who wish to be banned from the casino. If the person is discovered on the casino premises, they can be charged with trespassing. If they win a jackpot, the casino has the right to with-hold their winnings and deposit them into a Gambling Treatment Fund. The ban can be a good tool to help the struggling gambler, but it's not the only tool. The compulsive gambler may also benefit from medical examinations and medications for physical, mental, or emotional diagnoses.

There's a century-old question about whether gambling is harmless entertainment. In gambling, one player wins at the expense of others. The bigger I win, the more the others have to lose. How can we ignore the clever advertisements, the free bus rides to the casinos, and the VIP treatment? Where else can I go where I can satisfy at least two of my addictions? They offer alcohol, allow smoking, and encourage gambling. It's an addict's paradise. I sometimes wonder how my life would have ended if there had been Indian-run casinos in Arizona when I gambled compulsively? Or if there had been Internet gambling?

Some recent newspaper stories relate tragic events where the gambler failed to win the jackpot:

- A former real-estate agent pleaded guilty to killing a loan shark with a meat cleaver in a dispute over gambling debts.

- A woman was charged with embezzling $1.2 million from her employer and blowing most of it in casino slot machines.

- A financial adviser bludgeoned a seventy-two-year-old woman to death to cover up his embezzlement of two hundred thousand dollars from her accounts.

- A town treasurer pleaded guilty to stealing 228 thousand dollars of taxpayers' money to cover gambling debts.

- A man who came home from Las Vegas distraught over gambling debts killed his pregnant wife and three children, then shot himself to death.

- A special report about the suicide of a county's top prosecutor revealed a man with deep financial troubles and a gambling addiction that threatened to ruin his political career.

- A gambling habit led to prison for a sixty-four-year-old man-

ager of a credit union, who got four years for embezzling 275
thousand dollars.

- A former police officer appeared in federal court to face charges
that he embezzled funds from the police department's downtown narcotics unit and spent most of the money gambling in
local casinos and at a horse track.

- A former deputy treasurer was sentenced to twelve years in
prison after being convicted of embezzling 197 thousand dollars over three years to support a gambling habit.

- An attempted casino robbery reads like a Hollywood film:
Four men planned an elaborate scheme to rob a casino of $2
million dollars, because they had lost money while gambling
there. They designed fake manhole covers and placed ladders
and ropes in the sewers for an escape, cut holes in the floor-
boards of two vans and parked them over the manhole covers,
and parked an all-terrain vehicle in the sewer to travel between
manholes. Armed with a 9-millimeter handgun, pellet gun,
smoke grenade, gas masks, pepper spray, cell phones, and two-
way radios, they were caught when they were unable to lift the
manhole covers.

- A woman faced a maximum sentence of eighty-five years in
prison for embezzling one hundred thousand dollars from a
state work program for the disabled.

- A woman says she killed her mother and husband as part of
a suicide pact made in despair over large gambling debts the
trio had run up at casinos. She testified that the three lost fifty
thousand dollars at casinos and decided to end their lives because they could not repay bank and credit union loans.

- But no one has lost more than the Army sergeant whose wife
left their ten-day-old baby in a hot car while she gambled for
seven hours. Their baby died.

One of the fundamental principles of GA is the concept that people with like problems can be helpful to each other and an example to each other. Beneath this principle lies a deeper one, which is that the help offered by GA can be effective only when it is asked for and open-mindedly accepted by the newcomer. Forcing GA upon anyone who has not "hit bottom" has been found to be a waste of time. The GA program does not conduct crusades for new members. GA is not a religious group, a medical group, or legal group, just members sharing their experiences, strengths, and hopes with each other. If a newcomer asks when to go to meetings, we tell him or her to go when you want to go, when you don't want to go, and when you don't know if you want to go. As long as I feel threatened by my addiction or fear of losing control, I can be sure I have not resolved the basic problem of my addiction. The fact is I must reach a point where I feel comfortable around addictions, like gambling, food, and alcohol.

The first Gamblers Anonymous meeting in Phoenix, Arizona, was held in April 1973. Eight years later, there were three GA meetings in the state—one in Tucson, one in Tempe, and one in Phoenix. The Arizona legislature legalized pari-mutuel gambling in the 1940s, but it was not socially acceptable for Arizona women to gamble until around 1981, when the state of Arizona entered the gambling business. In 1989, the state allowed "social gambling" in many bars and restaurants and games of blackjack, poker, and crap tables were available. In the early 1990s, the Indian casinos opened their doors in Arizona. Mike Brubaker was the only professional in the state who was qualified to treat compulsive gamblers. In 1993, Don Hulen and Archie Springfield made plans to form the Arizona Council for Compulsive Gambling (ACCG), and when Archie moved to California, Don invited Marvin Hamilton to serve as president of the council. The ACCG's organizational meeting was held on October 15, 1994, at the (now closed) Reserve Officers of Naval Services Club in Phoenix.

In 1996, Don obtained his National Training Credential, and the ACCG council conducted the first Southwest Clinical Gambling Treatment Training for over one hundred professional health-care providers. The providers came from Arizona, Cali-

fornia, New Mexico, and Nevada. More than forty professionals
received credentials as certified compulsive gambling counselors.
Don directed the council from his home until 1997. Several of his
friends volunteered to help collate training manuals for counselors
and brochures and flyers for distribution to gambling establishments. Funding for the council came from the Indian casinos. In
1996, the council established the second problem gambling web-
site in the world, and in 1997, Don moved the ACCG offices from
his home to downtown Phoenix.

For years I had believed that one person could not make a difference in any arena of life. Then I met Don Hulen. Don was at my
first GA meeting, and I later had the privilege of working for Don
and Marvin at the ACCG office. While working with Don and
Marvin, I saw many instances of the damage to the families of the
gamblers. GamAnon, the twelve-step program for families of the
gambler, has helped heal many spouses and parents, but children
are the littlest victims of the addiction, and they have no way to escape. Marvin, Don, and I, along with other GA members, traveled
to many small towns in Arizona and helped open new meetings
in outlying areas. Marvin has thirty-one years of recovery from
gambling and attended his first meeting in Arizona in 1975. The
Native Americans have provided over 95 percent of the funding to
operate the ACCG statewide gambling help line which was started
in 1994. The help line receives calls from thousands of desperate
people with gambling problems. At this time there are more than
fifty weekly GA meetings across the state.

After ACCG moved to its new offices, I served on its board
of directors and volunteered to help with seminars and presentations around the state. I still volunteer to answer the organization's
hotline once a week. In 1998, ACCG held its annual meeting, and
Don presented me with a plaque that read: "Gratitude for Giving Award presented this 27th day of February 1998, to Marilyn Lancelot, the Lady Who Changed the Face of Recovery for
Women." It was a humbling experience.

The ACCG should be recognized for its tireless efforts to help
the compulsive gambler. The council organized training programs
for gambling counselors, established a hotline for compulsive gam-

blers, printed and distributed literature for casinos, became a friend to the gambler who was suffering, stood by the side of many gamblers through the court process, and performed countless other deeds over the past thirteen years. I thank you Don, Marvin, and the Arizona Council for Compulsive Gambling for being by my side when I needed help.

It's been more than fifteen years since I started writing my story, and I still blink back the tears when I read it. After I stopped gambling, I found my Higher Power, and my prayers changed from "Please let me win a jackpot" to "Please help me make changes in myself." I can't go back and make a new start in my life, but I can make a new ending, and I thank God for bringing me to GA, and I thank GA for showing me the way back to God. I still go to meetings, write in my journal, rely on my Higher Power, and follow the twelve steps of recovery.

Today, if I am asked, "How does GA work?" my answer is, "Just fine!"

To quote my friend Lynne, "The best is yet to come!"